Brief Lives:
Elizabeth Gaskell

Brief Lives: Elizabeth Gaskell

Alan Shelston

Brief Lives
Published by Hesperus Press Limited
4 Rickett Street, London sw6 1RU
www.hesperuspress.com

First published by Hesperus Press Limited, 2010

Designed and typeset by Fraser Muggeridge studio
Printed in Jordan by Jordan National Press

ISBN: 978-1-84391-921-6

Contents

Foreword

In a famous letter of 1850, 'E.C. Gaskell', as she invariably signed herself, wrote of the problems created for her by 'my "Me"s [of which] I have a great number, and that's the plague'. That she should have been so conscious of the many sides of her personality shows her self-awareness, and it was typical that she should see her multiple selves as problematic. Her biographers have the same difficulty. Is she the writer who never lost her affection for the pastoral world of her childhood, and whose *Cranford* is still regarded as her representative text, or is she the novelist of social conscience, author of works of fiction about the challenging new industrial environment of Manchester? Are her novels primarily about social problems, or do they focus more upon the situations of their heroines? Is she the biographer of Charlotte Brontë whose efforts did so much to establish the Brontë legend, but whose sense of justice got her into more trouble than she bargained for? Is she the home-builder and mother of four daughters or the restless traveller who would often leave her family behind in order to escape the city with which she has always been associated?

The mixture of these various identities leaves us with our own decisions to take. Should we defer to the Victorian convention and call her 'Mrs Gaskell', as her early biographers always did or, recognising that this only seems to constrain her, refer to her as 'Elizabeth Gaskell'? This may seem to identify her in her own right; the problem is that she was hardly ever known by this formulation in her own time. 'Elizabeth' she was when growing up, but rarely after her marriage. To her husband William, she was always 'my dearest Lily', a diminutive that was also used by her closest friends. She tried to resolve her difficulties by saying that 'it's Wm who is to decide on all these things' but then, again so typically, she concludes, 'that does not quite do'. I shall call her 'Elizabeth' before her marriage and 'Lily' after it, since I think that brings us closest to the practices she would have recognised, and thus to the person she was. But above all I shall take her at her own word and explore the rich variety of all her 'me's.

The principal source for any study of Gaskell's life must be her letters, of which well over a thousand have survived. The bulk of these have been collected in *The Letters of Mrs Gaskell*, edited by J.A.V. Chapple and Arthur Pollard (1966); a supplementary collection, *Further Letters of Mrs Gaskell*, edited by John Chapple and Alan Shelston, was published in 2000. I have quoted from them extensively, retaining their sometimes idiosyncratic style and punctuation. I have not supplied precise references, but it should be possible to trace individual sources from the contexts in which they are cited. All quotations from materials held in the John Rylands University Library of the University of Manchester Library are identified and reproduced by courtesy of the University Librarian and Director. For a study such as this referencing generally has been kept to a minimum, but details of major sources are given in 'Further reading' at the conclusion of the volume. It is to John Chapple, friend and colleague of so many years, and to members of the Gaskell Society from whom I have learned so much, that I dedicate this book.

A Little Giddy Thoughtless Thing

Some time in 1811, towards the very end of the year, a baby aged little more than twelve months was taken on the two hundred mile journey from Chelsea, in London, to Knutsford, in Cheshire. Such a journey would have been arduous for an adult; in midwinter it would have been more than usually so for both adult and child. The baby was Elizabeth Stevenson: Elizabeth after her mother who had recently died. Elizabeth Stevenson would one day become 'Mrs Gaskell', the successful Victorian novelist who was always to be defined by her contemporaries by reference to her married status. The death of her mother was only the first of the experiences of loss that she would suffer in her life; Knutsford was to give her a new home and new sources of affection.

Knutsford, some thirteen miles from Manchester, was to be the centre of Elizabeth Stevenson's formative experiences and a reference point for her memory throughout her life. Here she lived with her aunt, Hannah Lumb, her mother's sister who had taken her in. Elizabeth would one day refer to her as 'my more than mother'.[1] Aunt Lumb's own life was not untroubled, in that she had been deserted by her husband and left as a single parent to bring up her apparently invalid daughter Marianne, who died, aged twenty-one, in the year following Elizabeth's arrival. Elizabeth's father, William Stevenson, at this time a government official, would seem to have kept in touch with his daughter, and she sometimes visited him in his Chelsea home. However, he had married again, and from a very early age Elizabeth must have become aware of the difficulties of fractured families. There was however an important unifying factor in her family circumstances. Her mother's family, the Hollands, were of firm Unitarian principles, while her father too came of dissenting stock. On the one hand the extended Unitarian networks led to distinguished connections through marriage to cousins far afield like the Wedgwoods and the Darwins; at a more local level they provided the assurance that brought the immediate families together.

Unitarianism is the broadest of churches. Originating in seventeenth-century dissent, and taking in the rationalism of the Enlightenment, its core belief lies in the principle of a single God, and the rejection of the concept of the trinity. As Elizabeth herself wrote to her eldest daughter in 1854, 'the one thing I *am* clear and sure about is that Jesus Christ was not equal to His father; that however divine a being he was *not* God.' Beyond this basic position Unitarianism prided itself on its rationalism. Its frameworks are at the same time closely defined and intellectually inclusive. It could tolerate, for example, a figure like the radical scientist Joseph Priestley whose rationalism took him to the point of atheism, while at the same time there were Unitarian clergy who were not so distant from the established church itself. It was above all a creed of conscience, but conscience rationally determined, and it was this that was to be Elizabeth Stevenson's inheritance. In her fiction she was to be the novelist of uncertainty, especially the uncertainties involved in arriving at moral decisions. She was equally a novelist who always worked within a moral framework.

Elizabeth's father himself grew up in a Unitarian tradition. Born at Berwick on Tweed in 1770, he was educated at the dissenting academy at Daventry, where Priestley had been a student, and later became a classics tutor at the newly established Manchester College, an institution prominent in the education of the Unitarian ministry. He was minister for five years of Dob Lane chapel close to Manchester before giving up the ministry on the grounds that he could not approve of stipendiary clergy: one suspects that this may have been a screen for deeper objections. He then turned to experimental farming near Edinburgh, and after that to agricultural journalism for the Scottish reviews before coming to London. William Stevenson's restlessness, both intellectual and geographical, is in contrast to the stability, and the financial standing, of the Hollands, from whom Elizabeth's mother came: they were mostly land-owning farmers, businessmen and successful professionals: clergymen, lawyers and doctors. Sir Henry Holland, cousin of Elizabeth's mother, was to become Surgeon to the Queen.

For its readers Gaskell's *Cranford* has always stood for her fictional transcription of Knutsford. In that sense it has become her representative text, and dramatic and television adaptations have reinforced that image. *Cranford* is often seen as a nostalgic work, representing a past memorialised by its author. In fact, with Dickens and Tennyson as the coming writers, and letters being posted in one of Rowland Hill's new post boxes, Gaskell's work represents, if only selectively, the Knutsford of the 1840s. Given that the town had no railway for another twenty years, *Cranford* can actually be said to be prophetic rather than retrospective. Knutsford, then as now, was a somewhat unusual town. Not exactly a market town, not exactly a backwater, it remains awkwardly situated with reference to major road connections. To the north lay Manchester, and to the west Chester, but access to neither was entirely easy. To the east and south lay good farming land; it was here that Elizabeth was taken to stay at the Holland family's farm at Sandlebridge, only a few miles away. Coming right up to the borders of the town was the great estate of Tatton, home to the Egerton family and also visited by Elizabeth as a child. Then, as now, the centre of the town was dominated by its massive Sessions House, built in the classical style in 1819 when Elizabeth was only a girl living less than a mile away. In its shadow was the gaol. Hannah Lumb's life was difficult, but she was not impoverished: her house overlooking the heath, even before its various extensions, was a comfortable one. At the very moment in time when Elizabeth Stevenson was growing up there, Jane Austen was living with her mother in Hampshire in more moderate circumstances. No-one would wish *Cranford* other than it is, but a more detached account of Knutsford in Elizabeth's early days is given in her essay, 'The last generation in England', published in an American magazine in 1849. Here she emphasises the hierarchical nature of Knutsford society, 'The daughters of [landed proprietors]... widows and cadets... professional men and their wives... shopkeepers... the usual respectable and disrespectable poor... and a set of young men , ready for mischief and brutality.' In much of its detail this account anticipates *Cranford*, but it is altogether a more clear-eyed view of life in a small provincial town.

Elizabeth was to spend her formative years in Knutsford, but this did not involve being cut off from her natural family. Jane Austen's Fanny Price reminds us that children at this time could be adopted by more fortunate family members when the need arose; the young Elizabeth's experience was not so unusual. Both her father and her stepmother wrote to her, and from the letters of Stevenson's that survive it would seem that he at least did so on a regular basis. A man with a commitment to learning, he concerned himself particularly with his daughter's educational progress: 'I hope you are again applying to your Latin and Italian; Let me know, when you write, in what manner you are spending your day – I mean as far as work or study is concerned.' Elizabeth was seventeen when she received this missive. William clearly had his priorities, and in the same letter he writes, 'Your mother [i.e. stepmother] will write... and tell you all other news.'

The letters that Elizabeth must have rejoiced to receive, however, must have been those from her brother John, of which enough have survived to suggest the very special nature of the relationship between them. Nearly twelve years her senior, John Stevenson was a 'free mariner' and in his letters he provides accounts of his own doings – parties when ashore and encounters with native tribesmen on his travels – while at the same time teasing his sister and admonishing her about her studies. 'What progress do you make in musick?' he writes, and to their Aunt Lumb, 'I hope you and everyone else continue to be satisfied with Elisabeth's [sic] progress.' The most exciting passages concern his adventures in India and Burma, where he is fascinated – and horrified – by religious practices, including human sacrifice. In *Cranford* the subcontinent would be the site of the adventures of Miss Matty's brother Peter, who like John Stevenson had taken part in the Burmese wars. John dutifully sends his sister a present of material from India to make a dress for herself: in the same way Miss Matty in *Cranford* receives a shawl from her far distant brother. John recorded his adventures in a narrative submitted for publication to Smith and Elder, who coincidentally published all of Gaskell's later works: his manuscript however was returned to him. The relationship of older brother and younger sister was very close, even in their separation: 'How I should like to have a stroll with you... when Elizabeth was a little girl of ten years old and liked her brother John to kiss her,' John writes. The affection was surely mutual.[2]

The education of the young Elizabeth Stevenson was clearly a matter of concern to everyone concerned with her welfare. Like most girls of her age and class she received the basics in the home. George Eliot, in *Middlemarch*, describes how Mrs Garth taught her children in the kitchen while she was engaged in her domestic tasks: 'She expounded with grammatical fervour what were the right views about the concord of verbs and pronouns with "nouns of multitude or signifying many"... in a general wreck of society [she] would have tried to hold her "Lindley Murray" above the waves.' *Lindley Murray* was the standard English reader of the time: in a scarcely disguised autobiographical reminiscence in her essay 'My French Master' Gaskell describes how 'we helped [our mother – i.e. Aunt Lumb] in her domestic cares during part of the morning; then came an old-fashioned routine of lessons, such as she herself had learnt when a girl – Goldsmith's *History of England*, Rollins's 'Ancient History', Lindley Murray's 'Grammar', and plenty of sewing and stitching.' French too she seems to have learned from an early age, from a French exile then living in Knutsford; in one of his letters when she was ten her brother compliments her on being 'forward… in French and arithmetic'. He, meanwhile, is learning the cutlass exercise.

The time came when a more rigorous scheme of education was needed. In her early teens it was decided that Elizabeth should go away to school, and accordingly she was sent to the Miss Byerleys, who ran a school of excellent reputation at Barford in Warwickshire. There remain some uncertainties about the precise dating of her attendance, but John Chapple leans towards Elizabeth's entry having been in 1821 in order to accommodate the five years that she would seem to have spent there.[3] In this case she could only have been eleven years old when she arrived. However that may be, it was both a good and a costly school. Again there were family connections: the three Miss Byerleys who ran the school were connected through marriage to the Holland family. Maybe this resulted in a financial concession; the fact that she was there for five years suggests that support was forthcoming. The school had moved to Barford from Warwick itself; during Elizabeth's period of residence it moved again, this time to Stratford upon Avon, where its pupils worshipped in the parish church made famous by its Shakespearean connections.

Education for young women in the early years of the nineteenth century was not simply an academic matter. This was the age of the 'conduct book' and conduct, in the sense of how a young lady should conduct herself, was as important as learning. When Elizabeth was about to enter the Miss Byerleys' establishment, she received from her father a copy of *The Female*

Mentor, or Select Conversations (1798), a work that gave guidance for both female behaviour and female learning. It recommended that young ladies might learn modern languages and the 'technical terms of art' – the emphasis is thus on the correctly spoken word – but that classical literature, in the original at least, should be left to the men whom the young women might hope to attract. Women, however educated, should avoid pedantry, since this of course would have the opposite effect.

By all accounts the Miss Byerleys' school was a good one, and it was attended by the daughters of a number of distinguished dissenters. The sisters themselves had Unitarian connections, although their pupils worshipped at the local Anglican church. The school had a library and, when it moved to Stratford, a ballroom of its own. Expensive it may have been for the minority of boarders there – there were day pupils from local homes but a prospectus written in 1810, before Elizabeth joined, advertises 'Instruction in English Reading, Spelling, Grammar and Composition, in Geography and the use of the Globes, and in Ancient and Modern History.' As well as this, 'extras' (because taught by specialists and involving additional fees) were available: 'The French Language, Music, Dancing, Drawing, Writing and Arithmetic.' Italian was later added, as were occasional lectures and physical exercise. In the early years of the school the enlightened sisters took their pupils on expeditions abroad, although Elizabeth's school visits seem to have been confined to the locality. On one of these she visited Clopton Hall, a manor house with historical associations, and more than a decade later an exercise that she wrote about it was to be published in William Howitt's *Visits to remarkable places* in 1840. Instruction in music seems also to have been a feature, since we have Elizabeth's music books dating from this time. Finally there would have been education in social behaviour, involving supervised attendance at parties and dances.

It seems clear that Elizabeth Stevenson enjoyed her stay at the school: in a letter of 1853 to Miss Ann Byerley, who had written to her sympathetically on the subject of her provocative novel, *Ruth*, she wrote with kind remembrance of her associations there. The village of Barford is named as the place from which her heroine sets out in *Lois the Witch* (1859), her story of the Salem witch trials, and it can be argued that characters and setting in *My Lady Ludlow* (1858) both have their origins in its author's school experiences.

Jenny Uglow has aptly described the Byerley sisters' regime as 'conservative, broad-ranging'[4] and such a description might equally apply to Elizabeth's wider reading. We know that as a young woman she read novels by Scott, by Susan Ferrier, and by some of their now forgotten contemporaries. She began Richardson's *Sir Charles Grandison*, but admits that she never finished it. We always need to remember that the Victorian novelists who came into prominence in the 1830s and 40s were products of the Regency before they became Victorians: Dickens, born two years after Gaskell, is a case in point. It is perhaps surprising that there is no direct record of Elizabeth having read Jane Austen when a young woman, though Austen published her six novels in the years when Gaskell was a child. In a letter of 1859 she told the publisher George Smith that, 'I was brought up by old uncles and aunts, who had all old books, and very few new ones.' If she seems to have been a somewhat random reader she was a re-reader of books that took her fancy and would quote from them instinctively when the occasion demanded. Writing to a new friend, Harriet Carr, whom she had met on a visit to Newcastle, she says, 'Fancy our agreeable situation not a book but which we have all read hundreds of times such as odd volumes of Hume, Shakespeare, Tasso and a few old newspapers containing our latest intelligence from the political world.'

Literary allusion is widespread in Gaskell's work: in *North and South* the individual chapters are headed by literary mottoes ranging from early ballads to the work of her contemporaries. George Herbert, Cowper, and figures like the now forgotten Mrs

Hemans and Mrs Barbauld are amongst the poets she cites. Perhaps these allusions are garnered from the annuals and keepsakes of the day, but it is clear from her choices that poetry was important to her, particularly for its emotional inferences. She would seem to have read Byron, even as a child when she sent an appraisal of his work to her brother and he reciprocated by quoting a stanza from *Childe Harold's Pilgrimage*, with the clear implication that she would recognise it. Later, as a young woman, she would read works as diverse as Mrs Trollope's *Domestic Manners of the Americans*, and Spurzheim's *Phrenology*.

In the years following her return from school Elizabeth suffered two great losses. In 1828 her brother John disappeared on a voyage to Calcutta. What happened to him we do not know: whether he was lost at sea on the voyage itself, or whether he just disappeared, leaving no trace, after he had landed in the subcontinent. The uncertainty must have intensified the pain of the loss. John's circumstances are reflected in major characters in both *Cranford* and *North and South*, although in each fictional instance the characters survive. What is strange, however, is that Elizabeth never referred to him in any of her extant letters for the rest of her life: he disappears not only from the face of the earth but from the narrative of his sister's life. And less than two years later his father William Stevenson followed him, in his case to his earthly grave. We have no record of Elizabeth's reaction to this second loss but for all the years of separation from them she felt close to both her brother and her father. Now all of her immediate family were gone. But there was to be no move back to live exclusively with her stepmother: she was rapidly moving towards a life of her own.

Elizabeth Stevenson entered formal schooling as a child, and she emerged from it, in 1826, as a young woman. She would have been welcomed back to her home with Aunt Lumb, but Knutsford must have had its limitations. To Harriet Carr Elizabeth wrote, 'I dare say if I went into the town I might meet two people, and if so I should return and say, "How very gay

Knutsford is to-day."' In the years that followed her return from school Elizabeth was often on the move amongst her various friends and relations. She would probably have made the first of her many visits to North Wales at this time, where her uncle Samuel Holland had established himself in the quarrying business; other relations were in Liverpool, where again we know she stayed. Of greater significance, however, were the approximately two years she spent in Newcastle, interrupted apparently by a visit to Edinburgh, at the home of the Reverend William Turner, a major figure in northern Unitarianism, founder of the Newcastle Literary and Philosophical Society and minister, scientist, moralist and progressive thinker. In both Newcastle and Edinburgh she would have met figures familiar with her father's habits of mind, while living in Turner's household would have introduced her to what might be expected of a clergyman's wife.

By the time of her twenty-first birthday in 1831, when she returned to Knutsford, Elizabeth Stevenson was a much-travelled young woman, at least within the British Isles. She had achieved an increasing sense of her own independence, and was now a very social creature. In Newcastle she made numerous friends, amongst them Harriet Carr, who lived very close to the Turners, and whose company she might have preferred to that of Turner's own daughter of a similar age. Harriet clearly provided the gaiety of spirit that was perhaps not to be found under Turner's roof: 'I have none to remind me of *Harriet Carr,* and giddiness (synonyms) but a great grey parrot the tones of whose voice sometimes resemble yours,' she writes from Liverpool, after leaving Newcastle. Clearly she very much missed her '*mia cara*', her newly acquired friend.

The five letters that we have from Elizabeth to Harriet Carr, dating from June 1831 to August 1832, can fairly be said to be more than letters in that they represent Elizabeth Stevenson's earliest sequence of narrative writing. Her brother John once told her that 'you have a talent for letter writing' and this is borne out by the huge body of letters that we now have available to us. With these she joins that group of writers whose correspondence can be said to equate in interest to their works. At the same time this treasure hoard can distort, since its record is inevitably incomplete. Nevertheless those five letters to her Newcastle friend certainly constitute the best direct record we have of her life as a young woman, and they lead us effectively into her later literary works.

What these letters reveal is a personality with instinctive wit, and imagination, pleased in everything, and more so everybody, around her, and with a very real social and intellectual assurance. She tells of going into a shop to get 'some coloured cloth' for some upholstery work and being astonished when the shopkeeper asked her if she wanted it 'for *Pantaloons*!' There is a half-amused, half-serious story about a Mrs Boddington, who was struck by lightning on her marriage journey: the brass point of her umbrella served to conduct the lighting via 'the steel in Mrs Boddington's stays' to 'a vital part in her leg'. There are balls and bazaars, parties and dances: we are in the world of the Jane Austen heroines. 'I cannot help admiring high blood and aristocracy,' she says. This is light-hearted, but it was to prove predictive. Above all there is wooing and marriage: 'What do you think of my knowing forty three *couples* engaged couples, not single people.' Another couple have taken 'four suits of clothes to be married in' as she comments, one for each season. But then, 'I never knew such a week as this for marriages… even more extraordinary I am not one of the number.'

Despite her disavowals Elizabeth's turn was to come, and perhaps sooner than she anticipated. Towards the end of the sequence she asks about a rumour, soon to be proved true, that Harriet is engaged, and then suddenly at the conclusion of the sequence, we are surprised by details of the arrangements for her own marriage: 'I am in the middle, or rather I hope, three-quarters through the bustle of wedding-gowns… I am to learn obedience on the 30th of this month… but I fancy to "learn obedience" is something new – to me at least it is... I smell marking ink and see nothing but E.C.S. everywhere.' As so often in her letters her high spirits interact with reflection, so that we have to know both writer and recipient if we are to tell how seriously she wants to be taken.

Elizabeth's husband-to-be was William Gaskell, junior minister of Manchester's Cross Street Chapel, in the heart of the city and with a good proportion of Manchester's dissenting business elite amongst its congregation. In all of Gaskell's correspondence, we have no letter of hers to her husband, and just one from him to her. The correspondence between them must have been destroyed by their daughters after their parents' death, much as Miss Matty destroys her parents' courtship letters in the 'Old Letters' chapter of *Cranford*. However, there exists a joint letter, dated 20th March 1832, from the newly engaged couple to William Gaskell's sister, excitedly (at least on Elizabeth's part) presenting themselves as a couple. Tradition has it that they met at the house of John Gooch Roberts, William's senior minister at Cross Street, and in a sense their marriage might have been predicted. A physically striking man, both in and out of his pulpit, William Gaskell had an excellent Unitarian pedigree: he came from an established Unitarian family in Warrington, where he attended the famous Academy. From there, like many dissenters of his generation, he went to Glasgow University where he studied a broad curriculum, including classics, philosophy, mathematics and science, and distinguished himself by winning a final year prize in Greek. Finally he spent a further three years at Manchester College, then in York, to train for the Unitarian ministry. Aunt Lumb was both astonished and impressed. 'Why Elizabeth,' her niece reports her as saying, 'how could this man ever take a fancy to such a little giddy thoughtless thing as you.' Prior to her marriage, on a visit to Edinburgh, Elizabeth had her portrait taken, an attractive miniature showing her glancing over her bare shoulder, her chestnut hair piled above her head and wearing a very full silk gown. It marked another rite of passage.

At the same time, also in Edinburgh, a marble bust of Elizabeth was made by the Scottish sculptor, David Dunbar. The two likenesses form a nice contrast: the one informal and free-flowing, and the other classically stylised.

In a letter written shortly after her marriage Elizabeth argued against protracted courtship, writing of 'the *wearing* anxiety of an engagement... [where] certainly one if not both of the parties suffer'. Certainly she did not suffer in this way although much later in life, where her daughters were concerned, she would seem to have forgotten her own advice. The wedding took place in Knutsford on 30th August 1832, in the parish church and not in the Unitarian chapel where she had worshipped since childhood with Aunt Lumb. The chapel, going back to 1674, still stands, an attractive brick building with external staircases to interior galleries. As a dissenting chapel it lacked the right to conduct marriages, although its burial ground is the resting place of some of Elizabeth's relations. The wedding was attended by numerous Holland relatives, and celebrated by the townspeople of Knutsford with a 'sanding' – the local custom of decorating paths and doorsteps with flowers and coloured sand. Elizabeth recognised this as a turning point in her life, and it seems to have been marked by the ways in which she was known. From now on she would always be 'Lily' to her friends and relations, and not 'Elizabeth', while she would invariably sign herself, even to her close family, as 'E.C. Gaskell'. For the rest of this biography we shall follow her example.

Marriage, Children and the Death of a Child

There is no new way to describe the Manchester to which the Gaskells came in 1832. With hindsight the timing was propitious for the progressively minded. In June the Reform Bill had been passed, giving the city its first Members of Parliament. The railway line from Liverpool was in its third year, providing a conduit for Lancashire's rapidly expanding cotton industry, and an easy means of transportation for people like Lily, with friends and relations in Liverpool itself. The system expanded locally, with lines throughout the north-west providing access to the Lancashire coastal towns, and the lakes. Later there would be travellers from America, notably Unitarian ministers arriving in Liverpool and crossing Chat Moss to visit Manchester's Unitarian luminaries. In 1847 Emerson would give his transcendentalist lectures in the city, and in 1850 Nathaniel Hawthorne was to take up his post in Liverpool as American consul there. In time Lily was to gain a number of American friends, but as far as we can tell these two novelists never met.

However, the cost of Manchester's development in terms of human dignity was severe. The summer of 1832 saw the height of the much-feared cholera epidemic. In that year James Kay, a man who would later play a significant role in Lily's literary life, published two editions of his research pamphlet, *The Moral and Physical Condition of the Working Classes employed in the cotton manufacture in Manchester*. In the second of these he wrote of 'the dense masses of the habitations of the poor, which stretch out their arms, as though to grasp and enclose the dwellings of the noble and wealthy'. Friedrich Engels, writing in 1844, would emphasise the same polarities. The Gaskells always lived on the edge of the city, in walking distance of open fields, but the division between rich and poor, together with its consequences, were things that they would come to recognise increasingly as they took up residence in Manchester.

First, however, there was a wedding journey. For this they took themselves on a month's travel in North Wales, taking in Samuel Holland's house at Plas yn Penrhyn, always remembered by Lily with affection. Marriage had brought her new friends in William's sisters, Anne and Lizzie, and she wrote to the latter in her usual jocular mode saying that she had 'a *great* deal of trouble managing this obstreperous brother of yours... Mountain [sic] seems to agree with us & our appetites admirably.' A few years later she wrote again to Lizzie, recalling 'all my favourite haunts' from this honeymoon, and advising her to 'come down gradually from mountains; not at once from Snowdonia to flat Lancashire'. The health of both William and Lily was always to suffer from the Manchester atmosphere, a combination of factory smoke and damp. William was prone to 'spasmodic asthma', although curiously Lily thought the Manchester smoke good for his well-being. She certainly suffered all her life from periods of low spirits and exhaustion when she was in the city. North Wales was to be the first of a series of country retreats to which she could escape when Manchester became too much for her: later there would be the Lake District and the Yorkshire-Lancashire borders. As she wrote to Lady Kay-Shuttleworth in 1850 after visiting her at Briery Close near Windermere, 'The work appointed both for my husband & me lies in Manchester [but] I would fain be in the country & this last experience of country air has done me so much good – I am a different creature to what I am in Manchester.' Many of her short stories are set in these remoter districts and they reflect the emotional pull that they had for her. The contrast between country and city inherent in much of Lily's writing comes with a conviction born of experience.

They returned to Manchester, to the house they had rented in Dover Street, just off Oxford Road at the city's southern edge, William to his clerical duties, Lily to what she called '*formal* bridal calls'. 'Calls' were a formality for someone of her social status, although a fellow Unitarian recorded that from the outset she was not prepared to undertake 'congregational visiting' – the term suggests social visits to members of her husband's congregation rather than philanthropic activity – and neither was she prepared to be 'looked to for that leadership in congregational work that is too often expected of "the minister's wife".'[5] Good works would be another matter; apart from anything else this was an area where she could exercise her independence.

In a letter to her old mentor William Turner, Lily wrote, 'I like my new home very much indeed,' but given contemporary accounts of the city it is perhaps surprising that she also tells him that the part of Manchester in which she lives 'is very countrified, and is very cheerful and comfortable in every part'. In an early story about working-class life, 'Libby Marsh's Three Eras', she gives a view of Manchester from the countryside of Dunham Park, some fifteen miles away: 'Far, far away in the distance on that flat plain you might see the motionless cloud of smoke hanging over a great town; and that was Manchester! Old ugly smoky Manchester; where their children had been born, (and perhaps where some lay buried), where God had cast their lives, and told them to work out their destiny.' In her second Manchester novel, *North and South* (1855), Margaret Hale approaches the city on a railway journey from the Lancashire coast; the first thing she notices is 'a deep lead-coloured cloud' hanging over the city, 'all the darker from contrast with the pale gray-blue of the wintry sky'. Nearer the town she finds that 'the air had a faint taste and smell of smoke; perhaps, after all, more of a loss of fragrance and herbage than any positive taste or smell.' 'Smoke', 'God', 'destiny'; the terms define very well what life in Manchester would bring, and how she would respond. It would also bring child-bearing, and the death of a child.

First, however, there were to be other concerns. 'Learning obedience' would not be easy. William's commitment to his ministry was absolute, and his post a demanding one. It may be that his periods of absence lay behind the long letters that Lily sometimes wrote when he was away. Even if she claims to be busy, explaining that she is writing while sitting at a meal, or between breaks, the letters that she writes at this time do not necessarily suggest the weight of domestic pressure. Rather they are expansive, suggesting a need to get things off her chest. In a letter of 1838 to Lizzie Gaskell she begins with the observation that 'the sort of consciousness that Wm may at any time and does generally see my letters makes me not write so naturally and heartily as I think I should do.' She says that William's absence for a few days at Buxton makes her feel lonely but on this occasion it gives her the opportunity to write as she likes. This is a frank confession to a sister-in-law but we should not be too surprised at William's behaviour since it was not unusual in the nineteenth century for husbands to read their wives' correspondence: Charlotte Brontë would suffer the same constraints after her marriage. But the sense of frustration was there. Later Lily would joke that her husband's letters were always neat and orderly, whereas hers are diffuse and badly spelled to boot. It was a significant contrast between them. Aunt Lumb's surprise at William's choice of Lily was not entirely without substance, for William's academic reserve inevitably contrasted with his young wife's more liberated mode of utterance. His sense of humour ran towards puns and rather heavy-handed wordplay; hers was spontaneous and unpredictable. 'Mrs J.J. Tayler has got an impromptu baby at Blackpool; went there & lo and behold a little girl unexpectedly made her appearance and clothes have had to be sent in such a hurry. Bathing places do so much good,' she wrote in another of her early letters to Lizzie. Tayler was another of Manchester's Unitarian ministers: William, one suspects, might have had misgivings about a comment like that about the wife of a clerical colleague.

Soon after her marriage Lily became pregnant for the first time. This pregnancy ended in the stillbirth of a daughter in July 1833, for whom three years later she wrote a commemorative sonnet, in which she says that even if:

> *... in time a living infant smiled,*
> *Winning my ear with gentle sounds of love*
> *... I still would save*
> *A green rest for thy memory.*

Marianne, her first 'living infant', was born on 12th September 1834; she was named perhaps for Aunt Lumb's invalid daughter, although later her mother often called her Polly. Lily experienced eight pregnancies before she was forty in 1850. Of these, four produced daughters who survived into adulthood, while a son was to die in infancy. From the remaining three there were another boy who survived only a few days, and two further stillbirths or miscarriages. Much of this detail is recorded in a letter of 1856 to her old friend Harriet Carr, now Anderson, but elsewhere we learn of these things largely by inference. The sequence is not unusual for Lily's time but it makes clear just how heavy were the demands, physical, emotional and practical, that were made upon her in the childbearing years.

In the case of this first child love and anxiety were in equal competition. This is made clear by the diary Lily wrote documenting the first three years of Marianne's life.[6] Written purely for herself, it was not published until long after her death, but it is a remarkable record of a young mother's concerns and anxieties. Its most recent editors have pointed out that at the time when it was written an increasing number of baby manuals were appearing, much as now, and Lily refers to her use of them when puzzled by aspects of Marianne's development. She reveals herself as a very serious-minded parent, to the extent that every development in the baby's behaviour becomes a cause for concern. Ever watchful, she refers to 'my theory that when children at any rate, are irritable something is physically the matter with them', but in general Marianne is 'very sweet-tempered'. However, the child does not seem to have any idea of 'obedience' and later we hear of this two year old's 'wrong-doing that has to be corrected'. In fact, the diary tells us as much about Lily's own state of mind as it does about her daughter's development. Running through it is her terror that the child might be lost to her: 'Oh may I try not to fasten & centre my affections too strongly on such a frail little treasure, but all my anxiety, though it renders me so aware of her fragility of life, makes me cling daily more and more to her.' She cites instances of infant mortality, which was of course more commonplace in the early nineteenth century than now; furthermore she had already lost her first child, also a daughter. And behind her fears, in all probability, lay the knowledge that a number of her own siblings had died before she herself came into the world. Before the diary ends, she records the birth of her second daughter, Margaret Emily (always known as 'Meta'), in February 1837, but in May of the same year Aunt Lumb died, after a painful illness. Lily had nursed her, but was unable to be there at the last. All of these reminders of mortality perhaps explain the strong element of religious supplication in the diary. 'Oh may I constantly bear in mind the words "The Lord giveth & the Lord hath taken away. Blessed be the name of the Lord,"' she writes, continuing, 'I feel weak & exhausted with writing, or I had meant to write more. God bless my dearest child, and help her mother in her earnest endeavours.'

On Meta's appearance on the scene she is immediately compared with Marianne: 'I fancy she will be more clever than her elder sister, if not so gentle.' In other ways too she is 'totally different'. Lily always saw her children as distinct individuals, guiding their education according to their individual talents, but from the start the two sisters would have to get used to this kind of comparison. Marianne, who became gifted enough at the piano to play Beethoven sonatas, would one day have lessons from Charles Hallé, but Meta, who had teachers to develop her drawing and artistic skills, was always regarded as her intellectual superior.

The arrival of the children – Florence (1842), Willie (1844) and Julia (1846) followed Marianne and Meta – meant the employment of servants and the need for more space. First there was Bessy, engaged to help with Marianne as a baby. Lily became attached to her, as she usually did to her better servants, especially those who were involved with her children. In 1842, Ann Hearn, a young woman from the West Country, began her career of over fifty years as the Gaskell family factotum. There would be others, notably Barbara Fergusson who came to give the girls their early training, and whom Lily came to treat as a friend. But it was Hearn, as she was always called, who stayed at the heart of the family, looking after the children – and William too – when Lily was away, and sometimes accompanying them on their journeys from Manchester. Later servants would be less satisfactory, notably Anne, a cook who became pregnant, and told Lily that 'the man' had left her when she was seeing him all the time, and a gardener who drank. There were others; the impermanence of hired help was a constant worry. Now that there were children more living space was needed, and in 1842 they moved to another house in Upper Rumford Street, close by their Dover Street home. This was still small for their needs, but they would be there for a further eight years before arriving at their final home in Plymouth Grove, less than a mile further out from the city.

The expansion of the family seems to have led William and Lily to spend more rather than less time away from home, both individually and together. There were concerns for the children's health to add to their own, but there was also their need for their own individual space. In the autumn of 1839, for example, William spent ten weeks on the Continent, exploring Switzerland, and then Venice and Florence. Later a trip to Palestine was proposed for him but this failed to come to completion. Lily's forays were, initially, less ambitious, but she invariably sought out places where country or sea air might relieve the discomforts of city life: Wales, for example, always at this time the favourite location, and the Lancashire coast, where she went after the birth of Meta and the stress caused by nursing Aunt Lumb through her final illness.

William's visit to the Continent set a pattern for the Gaskells' habit of travelling separately and independently when the opportunity arose: this they would do for the rest of their lives. Lily notes that William had misgivings about their both being away from the children at the same time. Nevertheless they actively encouraged each other's plans and when apart were always most solicitous for each other's well-being. As time developed their preferences came to differ: William would be reluctant to travel abroad, confining himself either to their favourite holiday place of 'beautiful Silverdale' on the Lancashire coast, or to Scotland, while Lily later became increasingly keen on Continental travel. In 1841 they went together to Germany, concluding their tour in Heidelberg. On the way they took in the cathedral towns of Flanders – Bruges, Ghent and Antwerp – and then Aix-la-Chapelle. 'I know it's dull work talking about cathedrals,' she writes to Lizzie Holland, but she cannot resist recalling their 'sublime beauty'. The Rhine is a disappointment, perhaps because 'it rained cats & dogs', as well as smelling 'of the bones of the 3000 virgins' – Lily was attracted by legends, whatever their source – but the stay at Heidelberg, with its students, its parties, the music and dancing and above all the food, was a delight: 'first soup, then boiled meat & potatoes... then sausages and pancakes (no bad mixture) then RAW pickled fish & kidney beans or peas stewed in oil, then pudding, then roast meat and salad, then apricot or cherry open flat tart about 1 yd ½ in circumference & no joke such immense things; then desert-cakes [sic], apricots wild strawberries – then coffee.' Lily's account of this experience bursts with her capacity for enjoying herself while underlying it is a deep sense of the romance of the situation: 'splendid scenery, dark pine woods rocks, & the picturesque town, and noble castle to complete it'. She meets 'a Dr of Philosophie [sic] – grave, German & philosophical' – and a cousin of Goethe; her hostess has a house that is four hundred and fifty years old, its walls hung with 'Van Eycks, Albert Durers &c.' and a library with 40,000 volumes. English poets and writers had preceded her as recent visitors, and the conversation was 'so high-toned & so superior'. Lily always responded with enthusiasm to new experiences, and this she combined with a fascination with strange customs and the lure of the past. Heidelberg met these needs in full.

Some time after their return to Manchester the Gaskells seem to have lost a second child, a son who died unnamed very shortly after his birth. In 1844, just as the loss of the stillborn daughter had been followed by the birth of Marianne, this unnamed child was replaced by the birth of another son, William, named after both his father and his grandfather, but always called 'Willie'. A letter from Lily to Lizzie written in the summer of 1845 gives the details of the family's domestic routine at this time:

> I have Florence & Willie in my room which is also nursery, call Hearn at six, ½ p 6 she is dressed, comes in, dresses Flora, gives her breakfast the first; ½ p. 7 I get up, 8 Flora goes down to her sisters & Daddy, & Hearn to her breakfast. While I in my dressing gown dress Willie. ½ p. 8 I go to breakfast with parlour people, Florence being with us & Willie (ought to be) in his cot; Hearn makes beds etc in nursery only. 9 she takes F. and I read chapter & have prayers first with household & then with children, ½ past 9 Florence and Willie come in [sic] drawing room for an hour while bedroom & nursery windows are open; ½ p. 10 go in kitchen, cellars & order dinner…

And so she goes on, right through the day until,

> Margaret (nursemaid) brings Florence's supper, which Marianne gives her, being answerable for slops, dirty pinafores & untidy misbehaviours while Meta goes up stairs to get ready & fold up Willie's basket of clothes while he is undressed (This by way of feminine and family duties). Meta is so neat & so knowing, only, handles wet napkins very gingerly.

Florence, Lily's third surviving daughter, was not yet three, while Meta was eight years old when this was written. Lily often made lists of this kind about her household activities, and she could turn them into art. If she conveys the extent of the demands made upon her by her household tasks she also manages somehow to relish them. Even in a domestic to-do list her enthusiasm carries over. William, she loyally records, while 'feeling most kindly towards his children, is yet most *reserved* in expressions of either affection or sympathy'.

Silverdale, a little village above what, in her story 'The Sexton's Hero' (1847), Lily refers to as 'the blue dazzle of Morecambe Bay', was to become a family holiday place for many years. They would rent a curious old tower to live in, and as the years passed they became on friendly terms with the local people. 'The Sexton's Hero' makes much of the dramatic expanse of the shifting sands in the bay, and many of Lily's best stories are location-specific in this way. Meanwhile the attractions of Wales still beckoned. The principality was becoming gradually more accessible, and wealthy businessmen from Manchester and Liverpool, attracted by the scenery, were beginning to establish themselves in grand second houses. At the same time Wales with its own impenetrable language, its traditional stories and customs, and its habits of dress, embodied for Lily enticing ideas of the remote and the strange.

In the summer of 1845 they went once more to Wales, to the country Lily knew well on the Llyn Peninsula, in sight of both mountains and sea. William and Lily, together with Marianne and Fergusson, formed the party, Meta and Florence apparently staying behind. Initially they stayed at an inn in Festiniog, close to Sam Holland's home, but here Marianne contracted scarlet fever, always a much feared threat to Victorian children. It could devastate families. A few years later Lily would be distressed by the deaths of three young cousins from the disease, and again in 1854 we find her rushing her children out of Manchester when she heard of an outbreak there. On this occasion, however, there was no avoiding it. Marianne recovered, and they moved on to Porthmadog only for Willie to succumb. He was not so fortunate, and after a short illness he died in Fergusson's arms. There was a terrible irony to his death: Lily had always feared the impact of Manchester on her children's health and taken them away from the city whenever she could: Willie had died in the very place that she had always associated with well-being. North Wales plays a major part in her fiction, in stories like 'The Well of Pen-Morfa' (1850), and 'The Doom of the Griffiths' (1858, but originating much earlier), and in the early chapters of her novel *Ruth* (1853). In each instance the beauties of the location are emphasised and every time they become the setting for tragedy. In 'The Well of Pen-Morfa' Lily wrote in a single short sentence, 'But the dead never come back.' Her contemporaries were accustomed to child death, and she herself to sudden loss, but that did not did not make it any easier to bear. She could truthfully say that she had no 'constitutional' fear of death, placing her trust in the belief that she would see 'light in God's light' – a quotation she often called up at times of bereavement. But she was puzzled by death, above all by its irrevocable finality, and her sense of the loss it created was overwhelming.

The stricken family returned to Manchester, stopping at Warrington to lay Willie's infant body in the burying ground of Cairo Street Chapel, surrounded by various Warrington

Gaskells. The choice would have been dictated partly by the course of their return to Manchester, but also by the circumstance that this was William's home town. William's stoicism must have matched Lily's distress. Several years later she wrote to her friend Anne Shaen of her memories of 'evenings reading by the fire, and watching my darling *darling* Willie who now sleeps sounder still in the dull, dreary chapel-yard at Warrington'. She continues, 'that wound will never heal on earth, although hardly any one knows how it has changed me.'

Willie Gaskell died on 10th August 1845. Gaskell biographers are agreed that Lily's response to Willie's death was to fall into deep depression, and that she was encouraged by her husband to write *Mary Barton*, the work that would bring her into public recognition, as an antidote to her grief. This is reinforced by an explicit statement of her own in a letter to Mrs Mary Greg, member of a prominent mill-owning family: 'The tale was formed, and the greater part of the first volume was written when I was obliged to lie down continually on the sofa, and when I took refuge in the invention to exclude the memory of painful scenes which would force themselves on my remembrance.' There were other factors to bring about her recovery, notably the birth of her last child, Julia, in September 1846 just a year after Willie's death. She was concerned too about William. A letter of 1846 to Fergusson instructing her about his diet after he has had a fainting fit in her absence suggests that she is back on family duties, and she gradually returns to letter-writing form: a long letter of March 1847 to her cousin Fanny Holland embodies much of her old buoyancy of spirit. Nevertheless, she writes at its conclusion, 'all those awful days are stamped in my heart, and I don't believe even Heaven itself can obliterate the memory of that agony.' It was perhaps inevitable that child death was to feature prominently in the novel that made her name.

Writing and Recognition

By Lily's own account in her Preface to *Mary Barton* she began the novel in 1845, when she was in her thirty-fifth year. She was thus a late starter on the big stage: at the same point in time Dickens, just two years younger, had completed six long novels. She could not have predicted at this point how their careers would be intertwined. Nevertheless she was not entirely a novice. With her husband she had written a poem, 'Sketches among the Poor', which appeared in *Blackwood's Magazine* in 1837. It was strongly influenced by Crabbe and also by Wordsworth, whom both the Gaskells revered. The previous year William had given four lectures on the poets and poetry of humble life; the spirit of Wordsworth lay behind this project as well, as it did a set of 'Temperance Rhymes' that William sent to the poet and which received his approval. Two stories of Lily's, 'Libbie Marsh's Three Eras' and 'The Sexton's Hero', appeared pseudonymously under the name of 'Cotton Mather Mills, Esq.' in *Howitt's Journal* in 1847; both were realist stories of humble lives. Prior to the publication of *Mary Barton* therefore there had been a decade in which the Gaskells had been active on literary enterprises.

William and Mary Howitt, Quaker proponents of what was then thought of as popular literature, were key figures in Lily's early appearances in print. The Howitts were indefatigable literary entrepreneurs; their works included travel books, popular science, and novels in English and in translation, all in the cause of the common good. In 1840 Lily's account of Clopton House had been inserted by William Howitt in a volume of his called *Visits to Remarkable Places.* The Howitts had encountered the Gaskells in Heidelberg and they had a strong investment in the provision of reading matter for working people. They acted as intermediaries between the inexperienced author and John Forster, reader for the London publisher Chapman and Hall, at that time Dickens' publisher, who offered Lily £100 for the copyright of the work. Lily was thus precipitated quickly into established literary circles.

Mary Barton was published anonymously in two volumes in October 1848. It was perhaps inevitable that the deaths of children should be the ultimate focus of working-class suffering in the novel: the hero, John Barton, loses both his wife and his infant son at the opening of the story while the deaths of two twins mark the distress of another of the novel's families. Lily cites a moving piece of folklore when she mentions a belief that a child cannot die while those who will be left behind are 'wishing it', that is, agonising for it not to go. It is usually argued that *Mary Barton*'s account of working-class suffering is also drawn from direct experience, but this needs to be qualified. Where John Barton is concerned, she is likely to have known of similar working men. Barton, whom Lily had intended as her titular hero, and '*the* person with whom all my sympathies went', was an example of the kind of industrious workman who in better times might have presented himself at one of her husband's lectures. Job Legh, the working-class naturalist who has learned from experience the limitations of political action, had his precedents in autodidacts like Samuel Bamford, a man whom Lily admired, and Richard Buxton, a shoemaker, whose *Botanical Guide to the Flowering Plants... within sixteen miles of Manchester* was published in 1849. These people were representative of a working-class culture with which the Gaskells undoubtedly came into contact, and which extended into the city's poorest regions. Lily writes of William's lectures being well received by 'the very poorest of the weavers, in the very poorest district of Manchester, Miles Platting'. Miles Platting, in the east of the city, had a rapid build-up of mills and factories in the nineteenth century, and the consequent density of poor housing made it notori ous for its squalor. However, Lily is unlikely to have explored the city's darkest recesses. She would have known where they were, if only to avoid them: most notably Angel Meadow at the back of Deansgate, mentioned in *Mary Barton*, and Little Ireland, by the River Irwell. Friedrich Engels was exploring these regions at nearly the very same point in time for his *Condition of the Working Class in England* (1845), although there is no record of the two writers ever having met.

In Lily's Preface to her novel she defined her priorities: they were 'to give some utterance to the agony which from time to time convulses this dumb people; the agony of suffering without the sympathy of the happy, or of erroneously believing that to be the case'. Those she calls 'the lowest of the low' are indeed dumb in her novel: only once in *Mary Barton* is there any reference to the Irish, amongst the worst sufferers of all, and that is only to the snatch of a woman's voice, coming out of the darkness as John Barton proceeds on his way to murder. The moment is one of reciprocal feeling, but Lily shared what was then a common antipathy to the Irish: some years later she wrote to Godfrey Lushington that 'the pure bred Lancashire man is a right down fine fellow, – it is the admixture with Irish that pulls [our people] down.' Lily's sympathy with her working-class characters in *Mary Barton* is undeniable, but they are almost all industrious working men, who through the cycle of trade have lost their livelihoods. For all her skill in describing their plight, her day-to-day understanding, as distinct from her sympathy, lay not with the working people, but with the Carson family, the employers, with their comfortable house, their servants, and their leisure time devoted to cultural activities. It is the Gaskells' own class who need to learn the lesson she teaches.

When she takes us into the Carson home, we enter what for her would have been familiar surroundings.

That being said, there is Mary Barton herself, a young woman of spirit, who from the moment she sets out for Liverpool to save her falsely accused lover begins a new life. Mary is the first of Lily's heroines to be faced with daunting responsibilities and desperate choices. By this time Lily's oldest daughter was entering her teens; it is fair to say that she knew more about the emotional dynamics of young women than she did about the slum districts of Manchester or the psychology of murder. Lily always insisted that John Barton, Mary's father, was the central figure of the novel. 'Nothing was real in M. Barton, but the character of John Barton,' she wrote, '... he was my hero, *the* person with whom all my sympathies went.' Nevertheless, she changed her title to identify the daughter rather than the father, compensating by changing the subtitle from 'A Manchester Love Story' to 'A Tale of Manchester Life'. Titles are significant in the marketing of any work of fiction; this was not the last time she would have second thoughts. The same conflict would arise over *North and South*, which she always referred to as 'Margaret', and henceforward most of her novels – *Ruth*, *Sylvia's Lovers*, *Cousin Phillis*, *Wives and Daughters* – would all be named with their heroines in mind.

For a first novel, published anonymously, *Mary Barton* achieved remarkable success. It was noticed, extensively and usually generously, by the major literary reviews. John Forster followed his initial recommendation of the book with a long review in *The Examiner*, observing that, 'We defy anyone to read *Mary Barton* without a more thoughtful sense of what is due to the poor.' In *The Athenaeum* the respected reviewer Henry Fothergill Chorley wrote that, 'We have met with few pictures of life among the working classes at once so forcible and so fair as "Mary Barton".' Closer to home comment was sometimes more critical but was rarely entirely unsympathetic; after all, Manchester reviewers could feel that they had direct understanding of the issues the novel raised. The Gaskells' minister friend J.J. Tayler praised the novel's use of dialect – the subject of William's annotations in the text itself, and of two lectures by him printed in its fifth edition. But, representing the mill-owning interest, W.R. Greg argued in *The Edinburgh Review* that *Mary Barton* risked misleading ignorant southerners about the real state of affairs:

> Were *Mary Barton* to be only read by Manchester men and master manufacturers, it could scarcely fail to be serviceable, because they might profit by its suggestions… But considering the extraordinary delusions of many throughout the south of England respecting the great employers of labour in the north and west… the effect of the work… might, in these quarters, be mischievous in the extreme.

There were other dissentient voices. The belief that God is a God of mercy and not of punishment was a central tenet of Unitarian theology. In a restricted sense Lily wrote as a Unitarian to Unitarians, and a novel that invited William's congregation to reappraise their Christianity – 'Oh! Orestes, you… would have made a very tolerable Christian of the nineteenth century!' – was not likely to be easily received. 'I have tried to write truthfully,' Lily wrote in her Preface to *Mary Barton*, but it was not the last time that she would find herself at odds with what was expected of a 'minister's wife'.

Once *Mary Barton* was safely launched Lily took herself off to Wales once more, to Plas yn Penrhyn, whence she conducted the correspondence that her novel had provoked. Staying with her there were two of the Winkworth sisters, Katie (Catherine) and Emily. The Winkworth family, five sisters and a brother, lived within a stone's throw of the Gaskells in a house later occupied by Mrs Pankhurst. Another brother had died when a child, of an illness contracted in North Wales: the coincidence would not have been lost on Lily. Susanna, the eldest of the sisters, translated works of German theology while Catherine, a devout Anglican, came to be a translator of German hymnody. Both were taught German by William. Lily admired their seriousness of purpose, although she may have found it somewhat overpowering, and she was amused by Susanna's unconcealed attentions to her husband: 'she snubs me so, and makes such love to William he says "my life is the only protection he has – else he *knows* she would marry him."' Lily was prone to premonitions that she might not live long and probably took this idea more than half seriously. However, they were close friends and regular correspondents, close enough for the sisters to have quickly detected the authorship of *Mary Barton*. Anonymity was soon broken more widely, both in London and amongst the Manchester circle. Although Lily's next novel, *Ruth*, was identified on its title page only as being by 'the author of *Mary Barton*', there was no sustained mystery about this unidentified authorship, as there was with the Brontë sisters. Lily professed herself to be concerned by her exposure, but there was little that she could do to prevent it.

The success of *Mary Barton* took Lily to London in March 1849, where she stayed on her own until mid May. She had previously passed through the city with William in 1847 on their way to visit more new friends, the Shaen family, when William observed that London's 'wide lighted streets were like Oldham Road in Manchester'. This was perhaps meant as a compliment, but Lily, ever responsive to new experience, found them 'much handsomer'. The family home of the Shaens was at Crix, near Chelmsford, close enough to London to be accessible on visits to the capital. They were a distinguished Unitarian family, the male members lawyers and the females educated to think for themselves, whether about politics, about what they read, or about the role of women. They can be added to Lily's group of Unitarian acquaintances who could be professionally useful to her: William Shaen married Emily Winkworth and became Lily's solicitor.

The longer trip to London, beginning in March 1849 and undertaken independently, proved to be new and rewarding ground. Lily found herself increasingly meeting intellectuals and conversationalists with lively opinions, but with whom she found she could hold her own. The most famous of her new acquaintances were Charles Dickens and Thomas Carlyle. To both she had sent complimentary copies of her book. Carlyle, for his part, thought it 'a book deserving to take its place far above the ordinary garbage of Novels'.[7] Dickens at first failed to acknowledge his copy, but then set out to cultivate its author, and Lily was invited to a grand dinner party to celebrate the first number of *David Copperfield*, of which she was given a copy. Here were all the Dickens set: Jerrold of *Punch*, his illustrator Hablot Browne, and John Forster, together with Thackeray and the Carlyles, man and wife. A visit to Carlyle's home was less successful, the Chelsea sage apparently being unaware that she had been invited; nevertheless he treated her to a typically Carlylean discourse. His wife, Jane Welsh Carlyle, described Lily after this visit as 'a natural unassuming woman whom they have been doing their best to spoil by making a lioness of her'; before setting out for London Lily had expressed her fear of being 'lionised'. She breakfasted with Samuel Rogers, the aged celebrity poet, and with Monckton Milnes, suitor to Florence Nightingale and collector of erotica: Lily would not have known him in the latter capacity. Charlotte Brontë had undergone the same experience in the previous year but endured it for a much shorter time. Lily was lionised but she was not spoilt, and she returned home to an excited family waiting to hear all about it.

Lily made new friends and important connections on her London travels. Dickens she saw most frequently, although friendship was never really the way to describe their relationship. But with John Forster she was to remain in affectionate contact, knowing that she could always call upon him for advice and support. And then there was Eliza Fox, an independent young Unitarian, daughter of William Fox the radical parliamentarian, and member of a group of radically minded women much concerned with the question of women's rights. Many of these women combined feminism with art. Lily was always cautious about the woman question, but it had already come up in discussions with the Shaens at Crix. Unitarianism in London had a different flavour from what she knew in Manchester, where it tended to be reinforced by the economics of free trade. Among those she knew, or would come to know, were Anna Howitt (daughter of William and Mary), Anna Jameson, novelist and art historian, and later Bessie Rayner Parkes and Barbara Leigh Smith. Howitt and Leigh Smith, who became on her marriage Barbara Bodichon, were, like Fox, painters. Another friend was Julia ('Snow') Wedgwood of the pottery family. The Wedgwoods were related to the Darwins, as indeed, if less directly, was Lily. Many of these were Unitarians and all of them, with the exception of Jameson, were younger than Lily; all of them, again excepting Jameson who had separated from her husband, were as yet unmarried. It is in the light of these new experiences that we find Lily keen to discuss the rival claims of 'family' and 'art'. It was Eliza Fox to whom she responded most positively. She usually observed the formalities in her correspondence, but Eliza quickly became known to her by her pet name, 'Tottie', and it was to Tottie that she wrote a series of letters in 1849 and 1850 in which she continued the discussions that had begun in London.

Immediately on her return to Manchester Lily informed Tottie that she had been met by William and then 'rushed upon' by her four daughters who 'almost smothered me'. There is a tendency to regard 'Mrs Gaskell' as the exception among the women novelists of the period in her domesticity: by this token the Brontë sisters, and later George Eliot, could concentrate entirely on their art. We need hardly think twice to recognise that this is an over-simplification where both Charlotte Brontë and George Eliot were concerned. Moreover, Lily was not unusual in having her married status recognised in relation to her work. There were Mrs Braddon, Mrs Oliphant, Mrs Craik, and later Mrs Henry Wood and countless others: it was in fact the norm to give married women their titles on the title pages of the books they wrote. Nevertheless, in domestic 'smothering' lay the problem for the discussion of women's rights.

Lily clearly felt free to discuss the problematics of her situation with her new friend. Her letters to Tottie show all her liveliness of mind, as she jumps from accounts of the Oxford theologian, Francis Newman, whose wife 'is a Plymouth Brother and *very* Calvinistic', to seeing the actor William Charles Macready 'in King Lear and out of King Lear', and to speculations about the authorship of *Jane Eyre* and *Shirley*. Lily was fascinated by people, and by the variety of life that they represented. But family always intervenes: when she invites Tottie to Manchester in November 1849, she asks her if she is prepared 'for four girls in and out continually, interrupting the most interesting conversation with enquiries respecting lessons, work, etc.' 'The girls *are* very nice ones,' she adds, and when she later had access to Charlotte Brontë's correspondence for her biography of her fellow author, she was amused to find that Charlotte had referred to her 'four little girls – all more or less pretty and intelligent'.[8]

Any visitor to Plymouth Grove would be exposed to the full range of family activity. Eventually Lily approached the issue head on. In response to a letter from Tottie about 'home duties and individual life' she writes, 'If you were here we cd talk about it so well... One thing is clear, *Women*, must give up living an artist's life if home duties are to be paramount. It is different with men, whose home duties are so small a part of their life. However we are talking of women.' But then she continues, 'I am sure it is healthy for them to have the refuge of the hidden world of Art to shelter themselves in when too much pressed upon by daily small Lilliputian arrows of peddling cares.' This is typical of her attempts to square the circle when confronted with conflicting demands. 'Home duties' must of course come first, but then 'Art' is brought back into the equation as a private place of retreat when home duties get too much. Tottie, like many other Victorian pioneers of feminism with whom Lily came into contact, was not faced with the problem, at least as Lily defined it. Of one thing however Lily was convinced: 'If Self is to be the end of exertions, those exertions are unholy, there is no doubt of *that* – and that is part of the danger of cultivating the Individual Life.' Does she detect a destructive element of individualism in the liberated thinking of her younger friends? Certainly she was extremely cautious about where their thinking might take them. Some years later she wrote of Barbara Leigh Smith, 'She is... a strong fighter against the established opinions of the world – which always goes against my – what shall I call it? – *taste* – (that is not the word,) but I can't help admiring her noble bravery, and respecting – while I don't personally *like* her.' The struggle to find the right word, the attempt to reconcile conflicting positions, are typical, but so is the conclusion, 'I don't personally *like* her.' For Lily the personal would always take precedence over the political.

The year 1850 was one of increasing activity on Lily's part, in terms of both her literary activities and her travels. In March she published her story 'Lizzie Leigh' in Dickens' new periodical, *Household Words*. This began a professional association with Dickens that would last for more than a decade. Then, in June, the Gaskells once more moved house. And in August Lily would meet Charlotte Brontë, who would become 'my dear friend', and the subject of her most problematic work.

The first number of *Household Words* appeared on 30th March 1850. It was a product of Dickens' sense of mission, the belief shared with figures like the popular publisher Charles Knight, and the Howitts, that writers had a responsibility to inform and instruct a new urban and lower-class readership by providing stimulating reading matter, thus including them in the Victorian social project. In his 'Preliminary Word' to the first number Dickens expressed the hope that his journal would 'be admitted into many homes with affection and confidence; to be regarded as a friend by children and old people'. When he was looking for potential contributors he wrote to Lily, 'I *do* honestly know that there is no living English writer whose aid I would desire to enlist, in preference to the author of *Mary Barton* (a book that most profoundly affected and impressed me).'[9] Given his concept of the journal one can see how well Lily fitted its agenda, and she responded quickly and positively.

'Lizzie Leigh' took pride of place as the opening item of the new venture. A story of a young girl's fall after she leaves her family home on the moors for the city of Manchester, and of her mother's search for her, it concentrates very much on what Dickens called 'family affections'; it also follows Lily's agenda of exploring the boundaries of country and city. It was rather longer than had been anticipated; furthermore Dickens himself suggested that she change the ending. On this occasion Dickens ceded on both issues to his contributor: 'Your design as to its progress and conclusion are undoubtedly the best. The inventor's, I consider *must be.*' This would not always be the case. Her next contribution to *Household Words*, 'The Well of Pen-Morfa', published in June 1850, tells of a beautiful young woman who has been jilted. Her third *Household Words* story in this year, 'The Heart of John Middleton', is a tale of a wastrel's conversion by the love of a good woman; Dickens considered it the best of them. Finally, Lily concluded this incredibly busy year with a long story in the form of a Christmas book. Entitled, after much discussion, *The Moorland Cottage*, it is the story of an arrogant brother and his long-suffering sister: in its way the sibling relationship anticipates that of George Eliot's *The Mill on the Floss.*

Despite her relative inexperience, Lily dealt with Dickens with remarkable confidence. Where her work was concerned she would always be clear about her intentions and argue for them to be carried through. But while she was writing for *Household Words*, she was differently preoccupied – she was house-hunting. The Gaskells rejected several possibilities before settling for a substantial villa in Plymouth Grove, only a short walk away from where they had been living, but a residence of very different size and status. 'We've got a house. Yes! We really have,' she wrote excitedly to Tottie Fox. 'And if I had neither conscience nor prudence I should be delighted, for it certainly is a beauty.' Prudence was a lesser problem than conscience: the rent was £150 per annum and Lily jests that she might end up in the new Borough gaol. Conscience, though, was another matter: Lily fretted lest it was wrong 'to spend so much ourselves on *so* purely selfish a thing as a house is, while so many are wanting'. And this leads her into an examination of her 'me's – the 'warring members' of her personality – of which 'I have a great number and that's the plague.' How can she reconcile her 'Christian' self with her 'social self', and then with 'another self with a full taste for beauty and convenience'? She tries to solve the dilemma, 'by saying it's Wm who is to decide on all these things, and his feeling it right ought to be my rule. And so it is – only that does not quite do.' The letter is a famous one, and rightly so, since it reveals not only the many-sided nature of Lily's personality, but her own consciousness of it. It defines too her attitude to patriarchal authority – it ought to have the last word, but only with reservations that cannot be left unsaid. When the family finally settled in, the girls had bedrooms of their own and William had a study immediately by the front door where he tutored his divinity students, while Lily continued to write on the dining-room table.

There were more new friendships. In 1847 Lily renewed her acquaintance with Caroline Davenport, long-standing friend and chatelaine of Capesthorne, a very substantial country house some twenty-five miles from Manchester – 'such a *dame* of a lady', as Lily described her. Mrs Davenport was about to become, by her second marriage, Lady Hatherton: if Lily thought her something of a snob, she was pleased to have the acquaintance. It was at Capesthorne that Lily encountered another titled lady who would have greater impact upon her life.

This was Lady Kay-Shuttleworth, wife of the James Kay of the 1832 report on Manchester's working classes and now, through his marriage, Sir James with a hyphenated surname. The Shuttleworth family home, Gawthorpe, was some ten miles across the moors from Haworth, and once Charlotte Brontë's authorship of *Jane Eyre* had become common knowledge Sir James took it on himself to promote his neighbour in the larger world. In August 1850 he engineered the first meeting between Charlotte Brontë and Lily, not at Gawthorpe but at Briery Close, near Ambleside, another Kay-Shuttleworth home.

The contrast between the two novelists could not have been greater. Charlotte, the author of a novel with an outspoken and determined heroine, was reclusive and single-minded; Lily was gregarious, and always anxious about the effect of her fiction on its readers. Before actually meeting Charlotte Lily must have had a long session with her hostess, who gave her some insight, albeit not entirely accurate, into the Brontë story. Left alone together the two authors 'differed about almost everything'; Charlotte, whose hero was the Duke of Wellington, thought Lily a 'democrat', but this did not undermine the rapport between them. The outcome of all this was a long letter from Lily to Catherine Winkworth, which outlined Charlotte's entire history almost exactly as she would record it in the biography of Charlotte Brontë that she wrote after Charlotte's death some six years later. 'Such a life as Miss B's I never heard of before,' she writes in her letter, and then goes on to describe the remoteness of Haworth; the eccentricities of Charlotte's father; the deaths of the mother and the first two Brontë children; the misery of Cowan Bridge school; the stay in Brussels, and the writing and publication of *Jane Eyre*. 'All this lady K S told me,' she says, without the slightest awareness that this might be privileged information, and some of it mere gossip. She wasted no time in repeating these details in letters to other friends; she could never resist the lure of storytelling, and here she had a story of a quite different kind from the one that had brought her fame. After her meeting at Briery Close, Lily called at another Lakeland home, Fox How, home of the Arnold family. Here Mrs Mary Arnold, widow of the famous Rugby headmaster Thomas, sat among a circle very different from that of the Kay-Shuttleworths; it included the Wordsworth family; there were also the Davys, relations of the famous Sir Humphrey, and the elderly Mrs Elizabeth Fletcher, an Edinburgh friend who had known Lily's father. Here the atmosphere was intellectual and quietist. Lily once wrote that she always felt restored to tranquillity after a spell in this community.

It was not surprising that after all this activity Lily began to feel the strain. William encouraged her to get away from Manchester and she visited friends in Worcester, in Warwick, and then in Worcester again. But there was one last unlooked-for source of anxiety in this remarkable year. In the later part of the year Marianne, now sixteen, had alarmed her parents by becoming involved with an unidentified and 'detestable' man. Both parents wrote to him, but this only elicited the impertinent reply that 'he has not the remotest intention of relinquishing his determined object' and that Marianne was 'not a child in manners'. Lily thought this perception of her oldest child *'a great mistake.'* We can hear her snort of derision.[10] Marianne too, she says, sent him a note 'of her own free will' – it was 'strong' but *'very* badly spelt', nevertheless her mother thought it would have the desired effect. The Gaskells' solution was that a school should be found for their daughter, who until now had been educated at home. This involved more careful thought: it also involved further travel by the now exhausted Lily, who with Marianne ended up in London for Christmas. For Lily, the problems of reconciling the conflicting elements amongst her priorities were only just beginning.

Family, Fame, Friends

If 1850 was a crowded year in the Gaskells' lives, it was also a turning point. Lily was now a writer of reputation, made confident by the fact that her work had been taken seriously in metropolitan literary circles. The new house at Plymouth Grove gave her the family home she had always wanted; they could each have their own space, a factor increasingly important as the girls were growing up. The new home would allow Lily to entertain her many social contacts, while its ample exterior space would be a source of delight as she filled it not only with plants but with domestic animals as well. A pigsty was built, and a cow was bought, together with numbers of hens, and the children could look out over the fields then lying beyond.

The search for a school for Marianne, away from Manchester, was undertaken carefully. Lily rejected various possibilities as unsuitable before settling on an institution run by a Mrs Lalor in Hampstead. Here, as usual, Unitarian considerations were brought to bear, Mrs Lalor being the wife of the editor of the *Unitarian Herald*. Lily was warned that she had 'brusque unprepossessing manners', but she thought the school 'admirable' and was later able to say that Marianne had achieved 'enlargement of ideas' in her two years' absence from Plymouth Grove. In that Marianne was sixteen when she began there, Mrs Lalor's was probably more of a finishing school, devoted to turning a growing girl into a socially accomplished young woman, than an academic establishment. Negotiated absences in the company of parents seem to have been acceptable, and Marianne was able on occasion to accompany her mother on her extensive programme of visits.

Marianne's two-year spell in London did not release her from her mother's supervision. From the beginning of her stay Lily insisted that they write to each other every week, and that Marianne should not write 'such good-for-nothing hurried letters as you used to do'. If a letter failed to arrive on time there were expressions of concern and sometimes a sterner rebuke. Lily's letters contain comprehensive details of family news; sometimes she treats her eldest daughter as a confidante on family and other personal matters. With their stream of unceasing admonition, most of the letters from mother to daughter are very long, and we find ourselves wondering how Lily found the time to keep her side of the arrangement: it is not unusual for her to apologise for writing in a rush at the beginning of a missive of several detailed pages. The result of all this was that we have, if only from the mother's side, a remarkable account of the attitudes that could lie behind the upbringing of a middle-class young woman in the mid-Victorian period. In truth Lily was something of what we have come to call a helicopter parent, but at the same time she treats her first-born as the woman she was becoming, as well as the child that she no longer was.

Dress was an important issue now that Marianne's efforts on her own account could not actually be directly inspected. 'I was a little sorry to hear you were wearing your *merino* in an *evening* that night when Tottie drank tea with you. Either you are getting into the dirty slovenly habit of not changing your gown in the day-time, or you are short of gowns to wear a *merino* to tea? Which is it, love?' Lily writes. Later she suspects Marianne of affectation: '*Don't* call Shifts Chemises... As Mrs Davenport said the other day "It is only washerwomen who call Shifts '*chemises*' now."' There could be no higher authority. Marianne is warned against hypochondria: 'I fancy you will get yourself laughed at amongst the doctors if you go about complaining of every little ache or pain; as I told you before,' and she was vulnerable on more serious matters. Lily reacted strongly when Marianne expressed political views of her own: 'Pray *why* do you wish a Protectionist Ministry not to come in? Papa and I want terribly to know. Before you fully make up your mind, read a paper in the Quarterly on the subject of Free Trade and then when you come home I will read with you Mr Cobden's speeches.' In the same letter there is a firm rebuke for her having expressed her views on Free Trade while ignorant of Adam Smith, and again Lily makes the promise that they will read his work together. The return to Manchester must have been daunting for Marianne on this occasion. Her particular talent was for music, both playing and singing. Here again she was not short of advice from home, Lily constantly monitoring her progress, but when she did return to Plymouth Grove there was a Broadwood piano bought especially for her in the drawing room.

Lily's attitude to each of her children was, one suspects, very much dictated by the position that they occupied in the family. If Marianne was subject to what now seems excessive parental concern, there were also occasions when she was treated almost as an equal. Meta, two years younger, seems to have had a less intense upbringing. She too was sent to school to finish her education, not to London, but to Miss Rachel Martineau, sister to Harriet and James in Liverpool, early in 1853. Harriet Martineau was a controversial figure: philosopher, economist, novelist, feminist and enthusiast for mesmerism, she upset many of her contemporaries by her outspoken expression of her views. Charlotte Brontë, however, 'relished her irrepressibly' and Lily came to her support on more than one occasion.[11] James Martineau was a fellow professor of William's at the Manchester New College and may have been influential in the Gaskells' decision. Lily was confident that the arrangement would suit a daughter of whom she always thought as intellectually and artistically the most gifted of her tribe. From an early age Meta had enjoyed adult reading with her mother: Ruskin's *Seven Lamps of Architecture*, for example, which she was 'quite able to appreciate', she read at the age of fourteen. Meta had intellectual interests and clearly shared the 'artistic self' that Lily identified within herself and which would later bring meetings with figures like Holman Hunt and Dante Gabriel Rossetti. She was, her mother said, 'full of politics and water-colours'. Meta was not without spirit and once received 'a parental rebuke' for being 'a little too thick in the dancing line' with an officer with whom she had danced 'eight times in one evening'. A broken love affair lay in her future, but she was close to her mother and was to become her amanuensis as need arose.

As children, the two younger daughters, Florence and Julia, were often considered together. Again this was a matter of family positioning: there was a gap of five years between Meta and Florence. When Marianne returned to Manchester she took on the teaching of her two youngest sisters, the Gaskells being opposed to having a governess in the house. They then went to schools close to home. Poor Florence, Lily told her sister-in-law Anne Robson, 'has no talents under the sun' – surely a heavy burden to carry in this family – furthermore, 'she always wants to be one of the older girls,' and had problems 'in the temper line'. Things improved, however: 'pretty Flossy', it is recorded, 'went to two dances, and began to be a little belle'. Following the pattern of her elder sisters she did not go to school until she was seventeen, when she was sent to a school at Knutsford run by Henry Green, minister at the Unitarian chapel there. The Greens had four daughters of their own, together with a son who converted to Rome, and Green's wife Mary became a close friend with whom Lily could discuss such problems as the thoughtlessness of children and the constraints she felt as a minister's wife. Their friendship reinforced the Knutsford connection at a time when Lily might have felt she was losing it. Meanwhile Julia, who remained in Manchester for her schooling, was 'witty & wise & clever & droll'. She greatly impressed Charlotte

Brontë, who described her as 'a dangerous little person' who 'surreptitiously possessed herself of a minute fraction of my heart'. In that Charlotte believed herself to be a 'stranger' to children, this was a uniquely generous comment.[12] The 'talentless' Florence would one day make an excellent marriage, and dine with Henry James, while Julia would later have a mind very much of her own, but these developments – apart from Florence's marriage – their mother would not live to see.

Marianne's removal to London provided Lily with another pretext for visits to the capital. In 1851 she went three times to the Great Exhibition, in spite of her dislike of it; she left it to William, who was more enthusiastic, to take Marianne. She often combined her London excursions with country house visits to friends in the south of England, like the Shaens in Essex, or the Duckworth family in Southampton. When away she invariably stayed with friends; this was socially agreeable but of course it necessitated reciprocal arrangements, and when she returned to Plymouth Grove she often found herself preparing to receive visitors of her own. After one such excursion in 1849 she wrote to Tottie Fox, describing being met by William – '6 feet tall, thin hair inclined to grey' – and telling him and the girls all she has done while away in London: 'All six husband wife and children four talked at once,' she says, '... my ancles [sic] ached with talking at the end of the day.' Times could be particularly stressful when there were events in Manchester that attracted visitors: in September 1852, for example, when Dickens visited the city to speak at the opening of the Central Library, he and his wife called at Plymouth Grove, arranging for Lily to attend the ceremony, an exhausting seven-hour performance with 'speeches so long I could not attend & wished myself at home many & many a time'. The following evening there was a birthday party for the six-year-old Julia: there is something very modern about this struggle to combine personal and family activities.

It was soon after this that Lily made the first of what were to be frequent visits to France, usually to Paris, where she became a friend of Mme Mohl, a Francophile Englishwoman who had established herself at the centre of a salon. William, with Marianne, accompanied her on the first of these visits in May 1853. On their return Lily attended a grand dinner party in London with 'Macaulay, Hallam, Sir Francis Palgrave and Lord Campbell'. Lord Campbell was the Lord Chancellor of England: Lily always enjoyed the company of lawyers but cannot have expected to meet one as distinguished as this. Macaulay, Hallam and Palgrave had also trained as lawyers but by this time were known for both their literary prowess and their social standing. This was followed by 'another great dinner' at Lady Coltman's, where Sir Charles and Lady Trevelyan, the Monckton Milneses and the Dean of St Paul's were present. William, no doubt relieved to be able to excuse himself from all this grandeur, had returned to Manchester, and Marianne was praised for looking after him. Lily now had entrée to very exclusive circles, and titled connections appear increasingly in her correspondence. Later too there would be bishops and heads of Oxford houses amongst her acquaintance, and one day there would be the Duke of Devonshire, rather surprisingly addressed as 'Dear Duke'.

Throughout the rest of Lily's life she visited France both with and without her family whenever her schedule made it possible to do so. She enjoyed Mme Mohl's salon both for the intellectual stimulus it provided and for the way it called up the style of a previous age. There was also an ethical dimension: Florence Nightingale had been there after visiting the nursing order at Kaiserswerth in Germany, just before Lily's first visit. This was an interest of both Lily and the Winkworth women. Lily however would have to wait a little longer before meeting Nightingale face to face. Lily's essay 'Company Manners' (1854) draws vividly on her experiences at Mme Mohl's. She also travelled within France, to Chartres for example, where, as she says in her later essay 'French Life' (1862), she found the cathedral 'so wonderfully beautiful that no words can describe it'. Lily was Protestant to the core, but she also had a weakness for ritual and her Continental experiences provided her with the opportunity to explore its manifestations.

All of this travel took Lily away from Plymouth Grove for considerable periods of time; it could also be extremely stressful, a problem she would solve by setting off once again for her retreats in the Lakes. Lily clearly delighted in her Manchester home but Manchester's climate was never kind to her. She needed a great deal of domestic help and servants – with the exception of the ever-reliable Hearn – tended to come and go. Furthermore Plymouth Grove became an increasingly restless place, especially as William was now teaching students at home as well as at Manchester New College, the leading Unitarian institution. He was approaching seniority at Cross Street Chapel, and at the same time was Chairman of Manchester's Portico Library. He served on local committees too numerous to mention, while on the national scene he became increasingly active in the British Association for the Advancement of Science, attending its annual conferences whenever possible. Lily once remarked that she and her husband were like 'Adam and Eve in the weather glass' in that whenever one was at home the other was away. There seems to have been a suggestion in the early 1850s that the Gaskells might leave Manchester but William's work alone would have made that impossible. Lily might have wanted to move elsewhere, since she could never fully reconcile herself to life in the city, but in 1852 Catherine Winkworth observed that 'he [William] clearly feels that he has found the right place… Lily is proud that he is appreciated by people whose appreciation she cares for; so there is no more talk of leaving Manchester.' Lily, for her part, found herself increasingly involved in the needs of individuals: she sought financial assistance for the prison reformer Thomas Wright, and for Selina Davenport, a Knutsford novelist fallen on hard times. She corresponded with Christian Socialists, like Charles Kingsley and John Ludlow, seeking help for a Mrs Glover, dying of cancer; and with consequences for her next novel she sought help for a seduced young woman who had come to her attention. Lily recognised the toll that all this activity was taking. She determined on 'partly being by myself a good piece of every day which is I am sure so essential to my health that I am going to enforce it here', but inevitably this was a resolution that proved very difficult to keep.

Remarkably, Lily still found time for her writing amid all this activity. Dickens especially was keen for her to continue her contributions to *Household Words*. This she did, with an essay, 'Disappearances', about the effectiveness of police detective work, a very effective ghost story, 'The Old Nurse's Story', set in her favourite north country setting and another factual essay, 'The Schah's English Gardener'. Her most acceptable offerings for *Household Words*, however, were the nine instalments of *Cranford*, published at irregular intervals between December 1851 and May 1853. This was an arrangement Dickens would not have tolerated from any other of his contributors: the irregularity of Lily's submissions to him was due to the fact that she was at the same time privately working away at her second full-length novel, *Ruth*.

Ruth caused its author considerable anxiety, so much so that Lily seems to have kept the writing of it secret until it was near completion. The first instalments of *Cranford* were published in *Household Words*, in January, March and April 1852, then there is nothing until 1853. Presumably *Ruth* took over, since in October 1852 she reveals in a letter to Tottie Fox that Forster has given the manuscript to her publisher Chapman who has printed the first two volumes of it. 'I dislike it being published so much,' she wrote to Marianne. It is not until two months later that she says that it is finished: printing has thus begun from an incomplete manuscript, and this commits her to completing a novel about which she still has misgivings. The problem was the subject matter: *Ruth* is the story of an inexperienced young girl who is seduced by an older man and bears his child while he abandons her. She is taken in, with the child, by an elderly couple, a dissenting minister and his sister, who restore her sense of self-worth while hiding her past. There is thus a dual moral problem: is the fate visited on the fallen woman disproportionate, and should Ruth Hilton's protectors conceal her history with a lie? 'We are not to do evil that good may come,' the old minister who is protecting her says, but effectively the concealment is justified by the course of Ruth's life. Lily was increasingly anxious about the public exposure that the novel would bring. She was conscious that she had already written one novel that might be seen as provocative coming from a minister's wife. She herself described the subject of *Ruth* as 'inappropriate for fiction'. One suspects that she was also anxious about its effect not only on the Cross Street congregation but even within the walls of Plymouth Grove. She did say that she would read it with her daughters some day; at that time Marianne was nineteen and Meta sixteen, but there were also the younger girls to consider.

Ruth was prompted by a real-life case that Lily had come across of a young woman, 'Pasley', who had been seduced by a doctor whom she later encountered in the Manchester Infirmary. Lily was shocked by the case, and sought the help of Dickens, who had set up his Urania Cottage, a home for women in Pasley's situation. The subject of the sexual fall was a topical issue at this point in time; it figures in *David Copperfield* in the history of Little Em'ly, and is typified by Holman Hunt's picture 'The Awakening Conscience', first exhibited in the same year as the publication of *Ruth*. This was not the only time that it had surfaced in Lily's fiction: it features in *Mary Barton*, for example, and directly in 'Lizzie Leigh'. In *Ruth* it is central. Ruth's seduction takes place among the North Wales landscapes that Lily loved, and where she had lost her own child. Ruth is innocent and happy at the moment of her seduction in Wales, and we are expressly reminded that she had no mother to counsel her. The weight is then thrown on to the penitential career that is reserved for her. This is clearly a novel whose answers to the question it raises don't 'quite do', in Lily's term, but it bravely faces the issue and we can see why it should have caused its author such anxiety.

When Lily read the reviews her foreboding must have been alleviated, to some extent. For the most part reviewers responded generously, emphasising the double standard involved in such cases. George Henry Lewes found the heroine 'perfectly charming' and another reviewer went so far as to say that condemnation of the heroine could only be based upon 'a superstitious and exaggerated estimate of physical virginity'.[13] On a personal level reaction in Manchester seems to have been more ambivalent. '"Deep regret" is what my friends here feel and express,' Lily wrote, and she compared herself somewhat melodramatically to Saint Sebastian, 'tied to a tree to be shot at with arrows'. It is interesting though that *Ruth* is one of the few books of which Manchester's Portico Library, under William's chairmanship, held two copies: its issue books reveal how frequently they were taken out by its members, some of them members also of William's Cross Street congregation.

It must have been with relief that Lily returned to *Cranford* in the New Year of 1853 – no impromptu babies here, only the baby that Miss Matty dreams of in what might have been an alternative life, and which the servant Martha puts into her arms in the story's beautifully handled conclusion. *Cranford* was a fictional return to Knutsford; it had been anticipated by an essay, 'The Last Generation in England', published via the agency of the Howitts in America in *Sartain's Magazine* in July 1849. This was Lily's first publication in America; later her books would be published there just as they were published in England. A longer story, 'Mr Harrison's Confessions' (1851), can also be said to anticipate *Cranford*. A Cheshire story, it too deals with a town in which 'five-sixths of our householders... are women', but it has to be said that its development of this idea is much more crudely achieved than in the later work.

Cranford was originally intended to have been confined to a single story. This was entitled 'Our Society at Cranford' in

Household Words, and it told of Captain Brown's intrusion on the world of the 'amazons', leading up to his death, followed by the decline of Miss Deborah Jenkyns. The note of gentle pseudo-anthropology was entirely suited to Dickens' magazine, which often featured accounts of alternative societies; in a sense *Cranford* can be said to have parodied one of the journal's staple models. For its first readers *Cranford* was certainly not an idyll of the past, since most of its references are entirely contemporary, as is Mary Smith, the young narrator of the stories. What it offers is a response to contemporary society from the point of view of people brought up in the past. Dickens eagerly asked for more episodes; the result was the chain of stories that Lily revised and published as a short novel in 1853. For many *Cranford* has become its author's representative text, so much so that it can be said to have stereotyped her and inhibited appreciation of the wider range of her work. For Lily herself it was 'the only one of my books that I can read again' and it would be right to follow her identification of the humour of the work as the factor that has so much contributed to its success. A sense of the gently absurd had always been part of her own make up; responsibility may have suppressed it, but *Cranford*, like letter-writing, was an excellent outlet. Also in the completed *Cranford* we have the expression of a deeper sensibility, of opportunities missed, as in the 'love-affair of long ago' when Miss Matty was prevented from marrying Thomas Holbrook; of time having passed irrecoverably, as in Miss Matty's burning of her parents' love-letters; of the reality of real but unnoticed human suffering, and finally of the integrity of conscience that lies behind Miss Matty's determination that her failed investments should harm only her, and not those who can ill afford the loss.

Charitable giving was not in itself enough however. It was at this time that Lily wrote of the many people who would give money rather than their time to charitable work: such people will 'give tens & hundreds, that don't do half the good that individual intercourse, & earnest conscientious thought for others would do'. Interaction based on human sympathy was the message of Lily's favourite poet, Wordsworth, and of her favourite poem of his, 'The Old Cumberland Beggar', which contained, she said, the 'beautiful truth' 'that we have all of us one human heart'. This she cited in connection with William's lecture on 'The poets and poetry of humble life', and again in *North and South*. The humble life in *Cranford* is that of indigent old ladies rather than working men, but the principle remains the same.

Following the success of *Cranford* Dickens pressed for more material for *Household Words*. In 1853 Lily wrote a sequence of articles and stories for him on a range of topics. This kind of writing allowed for both reminiscence and experiment: she often draws on locations and ideas that have come to her on her travels, while sometimes the autobiographical element is patent, and sometimes it is concealed. In her essay 'Cumberland Sheep-Shearers', for example, published in January 1853, she retraces her steps in the Lakeland, describing its agricultural rituals in a way that clearly reflects her love of the region, while in 'Morton Hall' she returns to the Cheshire–Manchester axis, this time giving it a historical dimension by stretching her narrative out over three generations. 'The Squire's Story' is about a famous Knutsford highwayman: anecdotal and popular history was becoming something of a forte.

The most substantial of all of Lily's offerings to *Household Words* was her full-length novel, *North and South*, published in weekly instalments without interruption from 2nd September 1854 to 27th January 1855. At the outset Dickens welcomed Lily's proposals for *North and South* enthusiastically, not least because this new novel on the industrial theme would follow his own novel on the same subject, *Hard Times*. When Lily sent him the opening numbers in draft he replied, 'It opens an admirable story, is full of character and power... and has the very best marks of your hand on it.'[14] Fiction of this length was unusual in *Household Words* and Lily herself was unused to this mode of publication for a full-length novel. The pressure of serialisation, particularly on a weekly basis, was to prove considerable, and while she made sure that she was writing well ahead of the weekly dates of publication, she was always anxious about the progress of her narrative. For his part Dickens clearly decided to temper his initial enthusiasm with a very firm editorial hand. At the outset he made it clear that he would take responsibility for the chapter and instalment divisions. He was of course a very experienced editor and in a situation where precise calculations of wordage were required this, at least to him, made sense. But soon there were difficulties, and these are reflected in a key decision by Dickens when he decided to give the novel its title. For him, this was always to be a novel on the clash of cultures created by the new industrialism, the division between 'North' and 'South'. His choice of title, an echo of a speech by a workman in the novel, identified this theme exactly, and in these terms it was successfully received. But Lily's working title was 'Margaret', referring to Margaret Hale, the novel's heroine. What had come to the fore in the course of *Mary Barton*, the development of a young woman to maturity, was for her embedded in this second 'industrial' novel from the start.

Dickens and Lily became increasingly at odds, and nothing could really reconcile them. Dickens wanted economies, while Lily wanted more space to accommodate the resolution of the central relationship of the novel. At an early stage Dickens wrote to his sub-editor, W.H. Wills, 'I am alarmed by the quantity of *North and South*,' and he described the story as 'wearisome in the last degree'.[15] He wrote increasingly sharp letters to Lily to persuade her to conform to his requirements, although when the work was completed he tried to brush over the differences, by congratulating her and reassuring her that their disagreements were minor ones. But Lily stuck to her guns. When *North and South* appeared in volume form in March 1855 it carried a statement informing its readers that 'on its first appearance in "Household Words" this tale was obliged to conform to the conditions imposed by the requirements of a weekly publication.' She also took the opportunity to delete a quotation from Tennyson, inserted by Dickens to mark the industrial theme, while chapter mottoes were included and the final chapters revised and expanded in a way that allowed for the development of the heroine's inner consciousness following the crises of her life.

One suspects that there may have been a personal dimension to the conflict with Dickens. Lily had never been enthusiastic about him personally; she once accused him of 'stealing' a ghost story she had told and publishing it as his without any attribution to her. His attentions could easily seem over-effusive. Furthermore there was a tendency among her own social group to see Dickens as not entirely trustworthy, and this perhaps relates to his uncertain social status. In a letter of 1862 Lily asserted that 'half a dozen papers in H.W. are all I ever wrote for any periodical as I dislike & disapprove of such writing for myself as a general thing.' This was simply untrue: she can hardly have forgotten that she wrote two novels and more than twenty shorter pieces for *Household Words* in the nine years of its existence. She once commented on the grandeur of the Dickens' house, enquiring whether it was true that they dined on gold plates: the observation might have been in jest but one suspects that it was not entirely without malice. Nevertheless, Lily continued to write for *Household Words* and for its successor, *All the Year Round*. Her stories include some of her most interesting work, notably 'The Poor Clare' (1856), a story of an evil double which combines the historical, the paranormal and the macabre; 'My Lady Ludlow' (1858), an awkwardly constructed but effective story which takes in a narrative of the French Revolution in the process of exploring the subtleties of social change at the time of her own childhood, and *Lois the Witch* (1859), a story of the Salem witch trials that is in fact a psychological investigation of the dynamics of family.

North and South was Lily's most accomplished novel so far and it established her reputation as a novelist of substance: 'the best of

Mrs Gaskell's fictions', as a Manchester reviewer described it. Dickens paid her £250 on its completion and later she was able to calculate that it had brought her £600, taking into account its publication by the German publisher Tauchnitz for his series of paperback reprints, and its publication in the United States and, in translation, in France. Other works too went through these processes, and with William's help Lily now began to put the publication of her work on a more professional and financially effective basis.

It was while struggling to finish *North and South* that Lily met a Victorian figure who at first meeting astonished her: Florence Nightingale. In order to isolate herself from the demands of Plymouth Grove while completing her novel Lily had accepted an invitation from the Nightingale family to stay at Lea Hurst, their Derbyshire home, while they were away. She seems to have arrived at the point of the family's departure, although Florence Nightingale preceded them to London on the first stage of her journey to Scutari. There would thus have been little time for direct contact between the two women. Lily had known of the Nightingale family and they had friends and acquaintances in common, but this was her first recorded meeting with Florence. She was at Lea Hurst for about three weeks from September 1854, and her letters tell of the strangeness of her experience: as she says once the family have left and only the servants remain in the house, 'I have all the rest of the large place to myself... it will be very queer.'

In spite of this limited contact Florence Nightingale clearly made a profound impression upon Lily. In a manner exactly similar to her response to her first meeting with Charlotte Brontë seven years earlier, Lily could not wait to write long letters to her friends giving graphic descriptions of this new acquaintance. In a letter to Catherine Winkworth she gives an admiring description of Nightingale's physical appearance, adding, 'Oh Katie! I wish you could see her.' The account of Nightingale's character that follows is intensely religiose. 'She is like a saint,' Lily says;

a little later the saint is given a name, Elizabeth of Hungary. Another saint is then called up for reference: 'She seems as completely led by God as Joan of Arc.' In another letter to Amy Shaen Lily pays tribute to the conversations she has had with Nightingale's sister Parthenope, whose sense of her own existence, Lily says, 'is lost in Florence's'. She continues, 'I never saw such adoring love.' There are stories of Florence Nightingale's childhood, of her '18 dolls *all* in rows in bed, when she was quite a little thing', and of her childhood enthusiasm for Catholic legends and later for Egyptology, and then for the study of music ('the scientific part'). She quotes Florence's self-identification with Christ – '"I look to 30 as the age when Our Saviour took up his work"' – and she tells humorous stories that Nightingale herself told of her experiences dealing with drunken prostitutes at the Middlesex hospital.

There is one big reservation: Parthenope tells her that 'F. does not care for *individuals* – (which is curiously true) – but for the whole race as being God's creatures.' This may be 'curiously true', but in practice it led to a big difference between them. Lily writes, 'she is, I think, too much for institutions, sisterhoods and associations, and she said if she had influence enough not a mother should bring up a child herself; there should be crèches for the rich as well as the poor. If she had twenty children she would send them all to a crèche, seeing, of course, that it was a well-managed crèche.' For someone with Lily's commitment to motherhood – and for someone who had lost children of her own and her own mother as a child – that must have been impossible to take, but nevertheless her admiration remains.

'I think I have told you all – even to impressions,' Lily concludes. Indeed she has done, or as Lytton Strachey, future biographer of Nightingale, said in a different context, 'more than all'. What is so remarkable here is that, exactly as she did with Charlotte Brontë, she has based a comprehensive account on a combination of first impressions and hearsay. Both of these women were known to Lily for their achievements; neither of them, as far as we know, had she met before, and each time she is overwhelmed by the uniqueness of their lives and by the contrasts with her own. They were each of them, if in very different ways, opposites of herself, Florence Nightingale by what Lily called her 'unbendableness' and Charlotte Brontë through her depressive sense of her own isolation. Lily once reflected on the contrast between her own life and Charlotte Brontë's: 'Strange, is it not,' she wrote, 'that people's lives apparently suit them so little.' She would have welcomed solitude, at least from time to time, whereas for Charlotte it could be unrelieved torment. Lily took great happiness from every aspect of her very varied life, but she always had a sense of the road not taken, and maybe these two singular and single women embodied it for her.

Lily and Florence Nightingale later corresponded on topics of mutual interest. Lily also kept in touch with Parthenope: these were connections that continued to matter to her. But first came the war in the Crimea. The critic Henry Fothergill Chorley had begun a review of *North and South* by observing that it had been published in 'this year of war' and Lily, without perhaps realising the significance, had begun her novel by sending one of its characters, an army officer, to the garrison at Corfu, from where the first British soldiers would be sent to the battlefield. The Crimean war, like many wars, began optimistically, but as the full reality of the suffering of the soldiers became apparent, not least through the much advanced speed of communications and through developments in photography, the cost of the war was borne in on those at home. At first Lily joked about friends of hers who had gone out to the Crimea, as some wives did, to observe the war and support their husbands. They 'dress as Vivandières [caterers] & wash their husbands' shirts, cook each others' dinners,' she wrote, 'and say they were never so happy in their lives'. But only a short time later she writes to Marianne of 'poor Captain Duckworth much lamented by officers and men'. Captain Duckworth was one of their Southampton friends; he had died of cholera shortly after arriving in Bulgaria, en route for the Crimea. It was at about this time that Meta expressed an ambition to train as a nurse, an idea to which Lily responded cautiously but not entirely negatively by saying that she must spend some time observing hospital work before making up her mind. As it happened Meta's ambition ceased, and while she may have admired her daughter's motives, Lily, one suspects, would have been relieved

Despite her personal awareness of the cost of the war Lily never wavered in her support for it. Manchester had a 'Peace Party' led by the free traders Richard Cobden and John Bright, and Lily was convinced that their opposition to the war was misguided. In contrast she praised Lancashire working men like the 'fine-spinners in a mill in Bolton' who 'threw up their work and enlisted... on hearing of the sufferings in the Crimea, for they said they could neither sleep nor eat for thinking how the soldiers there wanted help.' Lily usually resisted any invitation to become involved in organised movements. She was always intrigued by the lives of the single women she met but while, for example, she signed the petition for the passage of the Married Women's Property Act, she had reservations about the women's movement itself. Later she would resist attempts to involve her in the anti-slavery movement in spite of the fact that some of William's close family were heavily involved. She mistrusted the rhetoric of public protest: 'I don't call the use of words *action*,' she wrote in 1859, referring to a series of anti-slavery lectures. These reactions were partly perhaps because of her public position as William's wife, but they were also due to an inherent conservatism – or to put it more positively a wish to remain free to keep an open mind on these matters. For his part William was uninhibited in his support for the war, preaching a remarkably belligerent sermon at its conclusion in justification of the doctrine of the just war and of this war in particular.

In a letter to Catherine Winkworth Lily once brought the two most famous single women in her life together: 'What would

Miss B. say to Florence Nightingale? I can't imagine,' she wrote. Lily had a number of unmarried friends and she sometimes seemed to envy them, but never to the point where she might seem to regret her own situation. She often weighed the pros and cons of the single life, saying on one occasion that she would not have wanted it for her daughters. With Charlotte Brontë there was no danger of being drawn into the kind of overpowering regime of commitment that Nightingale embodied. And Charlotte Brontë did not intimidate her. After that first meeting at Briery Close she made three separate visits to Plymouth Grove in the early 1850s, while Lily visited Haworth just once while Charlotte was alive, in September 1853.

Less than two years after Lily's visit to Haworth came news of Charlotte Brontë's unexpected marriage to her father's curate, Arthur Bell Nicholls, and then, seven months later, of her death on 31st March 1855. Lily heard of this from John Greenwood, a Haworth tradesman whom she had earlier pressed for information about Charlotte's life. She replies, 'I cannot tell you how VERY sad your note has made me,' but she then goes on, 'I want to know EVERY particular. Has she been long ill? What was her illness? You would oblige me *extremely* if you would, at your earliest leisure, send me every detail.' From a sequence of letters to Greenwood, and to George Smith, Charlotte Brontë's publisher, it is clear that Lily was herself considering writing a memoir of Charlotte, even before she received a letter from Patrick Brontë asking her to undertake such a task. This she forwarded to Smith, as a consequence of which her 'personal recollections' evolved into a full-scale biography for publication. Her response was that such a work would be 'a more serious task' than the personal memoir she had been thinking of, but she was 'anxious to perform this grave duty… well and fully'. Her anxiety did not prevent her from querying the payment of £600 that Smith offered for the work. This was all she had received in total from *North and South*, she said, and then there were expenses to consider. 'The amount of labour bestowed on the Biography (to say nothing of the anxiety in various ways,) has been more than double at least what the novel has cost me,' she later told Smith.

Lily's *Life of Charlotte Brontë* proved to be problematic from the start. As she wrote, 'I have to be accurate and keep to facts; a most difficult thing for a writer of fiction.' Particularly for this one, it might be added, with her love of the inventive detail, and the narrative strategies of contrast and melodrama. The Brontë story provided plenty of opportunity for these. From the outset it had been the strangeness of Charlotte Brontë's life rather than her literary achievement that had fascinated Lily, and to this she added a commitment to what she felt Charlotte's Brontë's history represented in moral terms. She went about her task with typical energy, seeking out details of Charlotte Brontë's life wherever she might find them. She questioned people in Haworth who knew the Brontë family; she visited Brussels, the scene of a crisis in Charlotte's earlier life, and she was given a cache of correspondence, albeit censored, to draw upon by Charlotte's friend Ellen Nussey. Unfortunately her research often stimulated her sense of the injustices encountered by her subject, to the point where her treatment of her material lacked discretion, and her wish to present her heroine as an icon of suffering led her to abandon all caution when dealing with those whom she held responsible.

A consequence of Lily's determination to draw a portrait of 'Charlotte Brontë the woman' is that little is said about her literary works: where she mentions them she tends to appeal to their public reception to make her points for her. Indeed despite her expressed admiration for *Jane Eyre* it is open to question whether she really liked the Brontë novels. At the very point in time of Charlotte's last illness she was asked to advise the French publisher Louis Hachette about suitable novels for translation. *Jane Eyre* she describes as 'a very remarkable book', *Shirley* she says is 'not so good' and *Villette* 'not so interesting'. About *Wuthering Heights* she is extremely cautious and in the *Life* she tends to see Emily's novel as another of Charlotte's trials. Emily, whom of course she only knew from Charlotte's account, seems to have been altogether too much for Lily, who once referred to her 'extraordinarily morbid development of talent'.

The Life of Charlotte Brontë was produced in considerable haste. Lily had been invited to visit Italy in the early months of 1857, by Mrs Emlyn Story, an American whom she had met in Paris. Emlyn Story was the wife of the sculptor William Wetmore Story, and the couple had a house in Rome much frequented by the American community there. But Lily was still writing the last two hundred pages of her biography in January 1857: once again she found herself under pressure when finishing a full-length work. The manuscript shows every evidence of haste, and the second volume in particular includes a large number of Charlotte's letters, copied out not only by Lily, but by her daughters and their friends. Heavy deletions on the manuscript suggest Lily's anxiety about her work: it is usually impossible to tell what lies beneath them. She received the proofs in batches, together with the relevant pages of her copy, and this went on almost until the point of her departure. Finally William was called into service. On 11th February 1857 Lily wrote to George Smith, 'Mr Gaskell says he will complete all arrangements with you: only as I have five minutes I just write to thank you for all your kindness and obligingness.' Two days later, without seeing the final publication of her work, she left Manchester for her most ambitious journey to date, a Continental journey that would bring her to Rome.

Rome, More Writing and the Final Project

Lily set out on the long journey to Rome on 13th February 1857, travelling through France via Paris to Marseille. From here she took a steamer for Civitavecchia on the Italian coast. With the Italian railway system as yet undeveloped, this was the only way to approach her goal. She was accompanied by Marianne and Meta, together with Catherine Winkworth and Emma Shaen; the party arrived in Rome on the 21st of the month. There had been a delay when the steamer's boiler burst, an incident later replicated in her novella, *A Dark Night's Work*, but when the voyage was resumed it was a great success. Marianne and Lily sang duets on the open deck while the sun went down and the rest of the party leant over the stern to observe the phosphorescence on the sea. They were joined in this romantic setting by a Captain Charles Hill of the Madras Engineers who, according to Catherine Winkworth, 'had known all the principal men in the Punjaub'.[16]

Once arrived in Rome, Lily was transformed. The Storys were the centre of an active American colony in Rome: they had taken a house for the carnival in the Via Sant' Isidoro, close to the Spanish Steps, and Elizabeth became a participant in their activities. The group also attracted a number of Roman Catholics, Henry (later Cardinal) Manning amongst them, and here the group of English ladies felt the need to keep their distance. On a later visit, in 1862, Marianne horrified her parents back in

Manchester by her interest in Manning's teaching; on that occasion Lily panicked and the result was a firm reprimand for Marianne and another course of reading with her father when she returned. This first visit though was unclouded by such problems. Amongst the Americans was Harriet Beecher Stowe, whom Lily had met and liked in England, although amongst her compatriots she was less easily accepted. Catherine Winkworth found her 'not popular here, any more than in England'. The Americans were all artists or writers of one kind or another, and in springtime, in the unique surroundings of the Imperial city, Lily was in her element. There were drives in the gardens, picture galleries and sightseeing, and there was Good Friday in the Sistine Chapel. In the evenings there were parties and dinners, and sometimes just ceaseless talk.

Before she left England Lily wrote to an American friend, Edward Everett Hale, saying that she could count the Americans she knew on her fingers. She then ran off a list of some twenty names. Missing from them was Charles Eliot Norton, translator of Dante and historian of Italian painting, but it was Norton, younger than Lily by some sixteen years, who was to contribute so much to her Roman visit. Norton was a Bostonian Unitarian of unimpeachable credentials. He had called on the Gaskells at Plymouth Grove some years earlier, in 1851, but it was not until their meeting in Rome that the rich sequence of correspondence between Lily and Norton, which has led some commentators to suggest that their friendship must have had more than an intellectual dimension, began. Their friendship was certainly important to them, but to imply that their relationship was in any way illicit is to misread the situation. Norton was high-minded in the extreme, while Lily was a woman of absolute moral principle who had just written a biography in which her emphasis on the wickedness of the dangerous liaisons of a middle-aged woman would get her into serious difficulties. Furthermore she was in a party that included her two daughters, now fully grown, who also became friendly with Norton. He for his part would continue to correspond with Meta, in particular, long after their mother's death. The mutual attraction between them was all part of the experience of release, intellectual and emotional, that each of them felt during this wonderful Roman holiday. There was nothing like this in Manchester. Like Lily, Norton was an ardent admirer of Ruskin, whom they both took as the ultimate authority on all things Italian; again like Lily he was receptive to cultural difference.

Lily and her party left Rome for the long journey home on 14th April, travelling first to Florence and then to Venice, Norton accompanying them, where they stayed for three more weeks. Unforgettably, they saw Torcello – 'Oh! that exquisite dreamy Torcello Sunday,' Lily later wrote to Norton, 'that still, sunny, sleepy, canal.' Returning via Paris, she did not arrive in Manchester until 28th May. Norton made his own way back to England. He was returning to the United States via Liverpool, and would meet the Gaskells again in Manchester at the great Exhibition of Art Treasures, an event that brought a whole host of visitors to Plymouth Grove, and which began early in May. There he saw John Everett Millais' evocative painting, *Autumn Leaves*, and when he encountered the younger Gaskell daughters shortly afterwards he remarked how they brought Millais' picture to mind. Immediately afterwards Norton left for America: Lily would not see him again.

Once Lily arrived at Plymouth Grove she found herself in desperate trouble. Her biography of Charlotte Brontë, initially a great success, had been under attack from individuals who believed they had been traduced in the book. First was the Reverend Carus Wilson, who had threatened to sue in response to Lily's account of the deaths of two of the Brontë children at his school. A more determined threat came from a woman Lily had charged with the seduction of Branwell Brontë, Mrs Lydia Robinson, now Lady Scott: again lawyers were brought into play. This Lily said was 'a horrid story', adding, 'I would not have told it but to show the life of prolonged suffering those Brontë girls had to endure.' But only two days before Lily's return retractions of her allegations had been published in *The Times* and in the *Athenaeum* on the authority of her husband, who had the tricky task of handling her correspondence while she was away. All the unsold copies of the first and second editions of the book had been withdrawn, and an undertaking given that the third edition would exclude the offending material. For Lily this was a dreadful blow. She had an enormous investment in this book as a tribute to her lost friend, and it was her conception of Charlotte Brontë as a victim of circumstances whose life was, in Charles Kingsley's words, 'made perfect by suffering', that had brought about the situation in which she found herself. She had fulfilled to the letter Patrick Brontë's injunction, 'No quailing Mrs Gaskell, no turning back,' reported by her in a letter to Ellen Nussey, and he had expressed his approval of her work both before and after its appearance. The severity of her strictures on those she believed to have been responsible for her heroine's troubles was exactly what had led to the threat of legal action. The alterations had to be made, and the third edition of the work, 'revised and corrected', appeared in August 1857.

There was then anxiety of a different kind. After the voyage out to Italy Captain Hill, their companion on the voyage, had attached himself to the party of English ladies in Rome, and he joined them in Paris on their return journey. Hill was a forty-year-old widower with two children. He seems to have made a good impression generally, and he attracted the affections of Meta, then half his age, to the point where, on their return to Manchester, an engagement was announced. An early marriage was contemplated, but William insisted on postponement. The Gaskells were far from happy about the situation, particularly as Hill was bound for India as an engineering officer and these were the early days of the unrest that was to lead to the massacre at Cawnpore in October 1857, only a month after Hill's departure. Friends of Lily, Lt. Col. Ewart and his wife and child, lost their lives at Cawnpore, and as well as the sadness involved, this would have brought home to the Gaskells the dangers of Hill's situation. Lily wrote to Norton, giving these details and saying, 'one's heart aches to think of India.' Attempts were made to find suitable employment for Hill in England, but to no avail, and his stay in India became prolonged. Initially Meta and Hill corresponded, but letters became less frequent. Misgivings about Hill's intentions increased and then it was suspected that he had been involved in some kind of doubtful behaviour, to which his family were obliged to admit. Meta broke off the engagement to remain, 'for life, as it were', in Henry James' words about his similarly maltreated heroine of *Washington Square*, at Plymouth Grove. Lily wrote two years later that Meta was at last recovering from her disappointment, but it was a distressing experience for all the family.

Meta's experience had demonstrated that the Gaskell girls were no longer children, and Lily began to see them more as a group of young women. 'My girls, my darlings *are* such comforts – such happiness! Every one so good and healthy and bright,' she wrote to Norton in 1860, when Julia, the youngest of them, was thirteen. Sounding more than a little like Jane Austen's Mrs Bennet, she continues, 'I don't know what I should do if any one of them married; & yet it is constantly a wonder to me that no one ever gives them the chance.'

However, ill health became a preoccupation of the family at this time. In 1860 William seems to have undergone a bout of low spirits: in May Lily records the fact that he is 'very flat, – I don't know what is the matter with him, he *says* nothing is, but he is in that silent depressed way, which is very unusual when he has been from home.' William took a month's holiday in Scotland, but this seems only to have been a temporary intermission. Eventually, in 1864, with the support of his congregation, he took his own trip to Italy, 'by himself, because he prefers it', Lily records, pleased to have been proved right when he 'came back a different creature, showing the advantage of change and travel'. When in Manchester

Lily frequently mentioned the headaches from which she suffered, 'which', she told Norton, 'are produced by the air of Manchester'. Her Paris friend Mme Mohl attributed them to a combination of the Manchester atmosphere, and the endless demands made on Lily's time: 'Mrs Gaskell,' she wrote in March 1863, 'had a constant headache for six months at Manchester, which went away as soon as she was here [i.e. in Paris].' She continues, 'her three daughters who are at Manchester are so worn out that their father means to send them away for a time.'[17]

According to Mme Mohl, who identified her work in the Manchester cotton famine in the early months of 1862 as the cause of her exhaustion, Lily suffered from frequent fainting fits. The famine was the consequence of the trade embargo on shipping from the southern states during the American Civil War; its impact on the Lancashire cotton districts, in the form of unemployment, was severe. Lily worked tirelessly with the Manchester Central Relief Office, organising fund-raising and the distribution of clothing, and her older daughters also undertook a great deal of charitable work. She expressed her anxiety about the toll taken on their energies, but nevertheless they persevered. Lily questioned Norton about the war in her letters. Her support for the northern side was unequivocal, but surely the southern states could simply be left to secede, she argued? As she writes to Norton, concluding a painstaking attempt to make sense of the situation, 'We have a proverbial expression in Lancashire, "Good riddance of bad rubbish."' Lily's concern about the war was intensified when she heard of the death of Robert Gould Shaw, son of one of her American friends, who was killed in action leading his regiment of black soldiers. First the Crimea, then the Indian wars and now the American Civil War: the cost of each of these conflicts had been brought home to her by the suffering of friends. Lily wrote a tribute to Shaw in *Macmillan's Magazine* in 1863, identifying herself with these losses: 'I, one English individual… know… of three only sons… living in happy homes, full of gladness and hope, who have left all… and have laid down their lives… to set the captive free.'

'Change and travel' was Lily's favoured remedy, and it took various forms during these years. There was a two month visit to Heidelberg at the end of 1858 with Meta and Florence, the latter claiming that her mother 'was like a mixture of a public house and apothecary's shop', due to her consumption of so much rum-infused cake, and of so many medicines for her various aches and pains. Maybe Florence was not without talent after all. Lily was again in Heidelberg in the summer of 1860. These visits would have reminded her of her first visit to Germany with William all those years ago. The second trip was more fraught, in that it involved keeping in touch with Meta, then on a tour of her own in Switzerland and France, looking after Marianne, who was recovering from chickenpox, and supervising Florence and Julia, the latter now 'petticoated' and on her first foreign journey. Fortunately Lily had taken the precaution of including Hearn, the ever faithful family servant, in the party. While Meta was on her Continental journey she learned that Captain Hill was engaged to be married; according to Lily, she 'seemed not at all troubled' by this news, but she continued to suffer periods of distress. The only letter that has survived between husband and wife was written at this time. It is from William seeking news of the party in Germany, and in particular enquiring about the details of the treatment prescribed for Marianne by her German doctor. 'The codine [sic], and bromine and iron sound promising,' he says, but he dismisses the idea of 'compressing the time of cure by taking two baths a day'. He concludes, 'I shan't be sorry when you are all on English ground… can you give me any idea of when it is likely to be?'[18]

In Lily's accounts of her foreign travel she invariably finds herself among English society, all of whose names she lists: it is as if, when travelling abroad, the English took England with them. There would be further visits to France, and in 1863 a second visit to Italy. She went to Switzerland with Meta in 1864, and to Paris once more in early 1865. William, meanwhile, when he was 'away on his wanderings', journeyed 'without any plan', so that she does not know how to contact him. One journey that was never made, although both she and William were invited, was to America. Lily was fascinated by America but although she tried to persuade William, she herself was always too busy to go. In a letter to Norton she conflates America and Rome: 'I have no notion what America looks like, either in her cities or her country or, most of all mysterious, her forests. Sometimes I dream I am in America, but it always looks like Rome, which I *know* it is not.'

So complicated was Lily's life in her final years that it is difficult to see how she managed to write at all. As she wrote to Marianne when working on *Sylvia's Lovers* (published in 1863), 'It is hard work writing a novel all morning, spudding up dandelions all afternoon, & writing again at night. Moreover I had a dreadful headache... And I have not got a cook... and am too squeezed dry of energy by the time I have done my book & my dandelions to see about either one thing or another.' Despite her differences with Dickens, and notably her disapproval of his publicising his separation from his wife, she had remained a contributor when, in 1858, *Household Words* had been rebranded as *All the Year Round*. Her first contribution was *Lois the Witch*; this was followed by 'The Ghost in the Garden Room', later renamed 'The Crooked Branch' for the 1859 Christmas number. *The Grey Woman* (1861), another longer tale, had powerful gothic elements. The short novel *A Dark Night's Work* (1863) relates aspects of her Italian experiences while, rather remarkably, 'An Italian Institution', published in the same year, is an account of the activities of the Neapolitan secret society, the Camorra.

These longer pieces all suggest new interests on Lily's part. Despite her prolific output she rarely repeated herself in her writing and was always prepared to explore new possibilities. With their hints of the sensational – crime, historical melodrama, the paranormal – these stories are in tune with the movement towards sensation fiction that was one of the fictional currents at the time. But also at this point in time there was a contrasting development in English fiction, the popularity of, in the terms of George Eliot's subtitle to *Middlemarch*, studies of provincial life. Such 'studies' invariably offered a muted but sympathetic realism and a careful depiction of psychological and sociological realities. George Eliot's own fiction, Trollope's Barsetshire novels, and Lily's final novels, all typify this trend. Lily was an unreserved admirer of Eliot's early work, but not of her mode of life. 'I should not be quite true,' she wrote to Eliot, 'if I did not say that I wish you *were* Mrs Lewes. However that can't be helped, as far as I can see and one must not judge others.' Eliot might have felt that this was judgement enough.

George Smith, the publisher who had commissioned Lily's biography of Charlotte Brontë, now became an increasingly influential figure in her literary career. Despite – or perhaps because of – the problems caused by the biography, Smith and Lily warmed to each other: he was a friendly and helpful man at the head of a publishing house, Smith, Elder and Co., which, if not new, had yet to establish itself in the mainstream of Victorian publishing, and she was keen to move away from not only Dickens, but also Chapman and Hall, the previous publishers of her work. Smith offered something different in publishing terms in both style and status. A businessman as well as a publisher, he had a very good sense of the market. In 1860 he launched his *Cornhill Magazine*, a monthly periodical that offered its readership substantial articles and quality fiction by the leading authors of the day, illustrated by equally distinguished artists. The first number contained Trollope's *Framley Parsonage*, illustrated by Millais. Lily thought it 'excellent & good & clever' and 'true and deep', and expressed the wish that it might never end. Cultural commentators like Ruskin and Matthew Arnold were also to become *Cornhill* contributors. Smith established sympathetic personal relationships with his authors, treating them as much as personal friends as business associates. This was something different from Dickens' flamboyant procedures, and while there was some overlap Lily had no hesitation in aligning herself with Smith. She was now, with William's help, taking firm control of her publishing affairs, investigating how she stood on matters of contract and copyright, and with these factors in mind she gradually made her existing contracts over to Smith's firm, negotiating with him over the publication of her new writing.

The first work Lily wrote for *Cornhill* was the ambiguously titled story, 'Curious if True' (1860), in which a visitor to France visits a chateau and has a vision of the traditional characters of fairy story. The story sustains the level of uncertainty embodied in its title – that is, 'curious' if it is 'true', or 'curious' but nevertheless 'true' – just as Lily seems to have been ambivalent herself about the paranormal, both in life and in her stories. This was followed by a tale in a German setting, 'Six Weeks at Heppenheim': Lily's travels were increasingly finding their way into her fiction.

Her first full-length novel for Smith was *Sylvia's Lovers*, published in three volumes in 1863. A historical novel set in the Yorkshire fishing port of 'Monkshaven', a fictionalisation of Whitby in the last years of the eighteenth century, it was in a different vein from anything she had attempted before. She visited Whitby in November 1859 to gather information about the whaling industry, and she consulted local historians about the area. Lily took almost four years over the novel, but again there was the usual last minute panic over proofs and publication.

Once more too there were uncertainties about the title. Initially the novel was to have been called 'The Specksioneer', thus identifying the focus as being on the harpooner of a whaling vessel, Charley Kinraid, lover of, and loved by, the heroine Sylvia Robson. However, this proved unacceptable, since the term might be incomprehensible to the general reader. The next choice was 'Philip's Idol'. This referred to the second male protagonist, Philip Hepburn, an ascetic suitor of Sylvia who allows her to believe that his rival has been lost at sea. Lily rejected this title too, and the focus changed once more when she adopted her final choice of 'Sylvia's Lovers'. Now the title was comprehensive in that it named the heroine and embraced both of the contrasting lovers.

Sylvia's Lovers is arguably the most emotionally powerful of Lily's novels. Sylvia Robson – like Mary Barton, and Ruth Hilton – is a heroine of humble origins, spirited but unlettered, who struggles to cope with the situations in which she finds herself. Lily is said to have called the book the saddest story she ever composed; it is perhaps no accident that it followed a biography with a Yorkshire setting of which the same thing might have been said.

The dedication of *Sylvia's Lovers* reads 'to My Dear Husband, by her who best knows his value'. However, when this novel with a heroine of divided loyalties was published in America, only two months after its publication in England, it bore a different inscription: 'To all of my northern friends, with the truest sympathy of an English woman; and in an especial manner to my dear friend Charles Eliot Norton, and to his wife, who although personally unknown to me is yet dear to me for his sake.' *Sylvia's Lovers* is about characters who find themselves troubled within marriage, and twice there are sobering reflections that seem somewhat imposed upon the situations they refer to. In the first Lily writes of Hepburn's discovery early in his marriage to Sylvia that 'the long-desired happiness was not so delicious and perfect as he had anticipated. Many have felt the same in their first year of married life; but the faithful, patient nature that still works on, striving to gain love, and capable itself of steady love all the while, is a gift not given to all.' Of another marriage later in her story, she writes, 'the course of married life, which should lead to perfect happiness, seemed so plain'; nevertheless 'resisting forces' make 'all such harmony and delight impossible'. These forces, she says, 'are but the necessary discipline here, and do not radically affect the love which will make all things right in heaven'. Of course Lily is writing here of her characters, in situations she has contrived for them, but there is something very personal about these reflections. There can be no doubt that Lily believed categorically in the indissolubility of marriage, but she is equally clear about the cost at which it might be achieved.

As before, she rewarded herself for the completion of her novel with another trip to the Continent, going again to Italy. This time Meta, Florence and Julia went with her, and en route Florence revealed that she considered herself engaged to an aspiring lawyer and son of a judge, Charles Crompton. Nine years older than Florence, Crompton had had a successful academic career at Cambridge. Lily was surprised, and concerned that Florence seemed very young, but any immediate concern that she may have felt was perhaps tempered by the fact that she had become very attracted by the university world, following a series of very happy visits to Oxford. Crompton's education was of the kind that Lily would provide for the Hamley brothers in her final novel, *Wives and Daughters*; and she had little difficulty in approving of him. Young, well-educated men seem to figure in her life at this time, especially if they could help her in her philanthropic activities – men like Charles Bosanquet, the earnest Cambridge-educated Anglican whom she met in Heidelberg; or the Lushington twins, Godfrey, Fellow of Oriel, and Vernon, a Christian Socialist, with whom she discussed social reform, Bach and Chopin.

Florence's engagement was a short one, and while her mother conceded that 'what gives them pleasure makes me happy too,' she admitted also that, 'I have had to take a good while to reconcile myself to the parting from this dear child, who still seems so much a child & to want "mother's shelter so much."' William conducted the marriage service in August 1863 and Lily conceded that the couple were 'thoroughly happy'. She also noted that Florence's 'new affluence of money makes her remember all the little wishes we have ever expressed', and that must have been a comfort. But she now found out how she would react when one of her children married, and her feelings were divided. She wrote to Florence Nightingale that 'the parting from a child *stuns* one; and it is very strange and difficult to turn back to the home-life and feel that she will never be there as before – as one's own *possession*.'

Any problems of this change in Florence's life, one suspects, were her mother's rather than her own. The pain of losing a daughter to a lover or potential husband is a very strong element in Lily's next work for George Smith, *Cousin Phillis*. This was a short novel, published in four parts from November 1863 to February 1864, with illustrations by George Du Maurier. The titles of all of Lily's last three novels – *Sylvia's Lovers, Cousin Phillis, Wives and Daughters* – focus on relationships, and the relationships are primarily those of courtship and marriage. But they also involve parents and children. Lily was conscious that a relationship between two people never operates in a vacuum; it will inevitably impact on those around them, and this she thought was never more true than when children marry, or when they leave home. As she wrote to her friend Mary Green of her son Philip's departure for India in 1860, 'I do not think he has an idea (when had children ever!) of how much you suffer at the prospect of separation.'

In *Cousin Phillis* Lily deploys the relationship of cousins as a narrative strategy. The narrator, Paul Manning, an apprentice railway engineer, is in his first employment away from home. He visits the farm of a relation, Farmer Holman, and there, for the first time, he encounters Holman's daughter, Phillis. He is nineteen years old but gauche; she is two years younger but assured – at least within the confines of the farm. The fact that they are cousins provides Lily with exactly the right distance between Paul as narrator, and Phillis as subject, for the true subject of the story is Phillis' emotional awakening, on account not of Paul, but of her love for his manager, Holdsworth, a man whose prowess as a railway engineer has taken him as far afield as Italy.

The unravelling of the story depends on a sequence of contrasts: the values of traditional labour, as against the new kind of work provided by the world of engineering; farming time, with its traditional rhythms, as against the coming of the railways which will bring a new notion of time and a new look to the landscape. The classical learning embraced by Phillis and learned from her father, who is indeed a 'whole man', contrasts with Holdsworth's linguistic facility learned on his foreign travels. Meanwhile Holdsworth will recover from illness at the farm, but at ultimately severe cost to Phillis' own well-being.

There is much here that has biographical implications where Lily is concerned. In a sense she was coming home to her own Cheshire countryside. The apparently idyllic Hope Farm, it is generally agreed, has its origins in her Uncle Sam Holland's farm at Sandlebridge. The references to railway building, both British and Italian, are historically accurate: the railway arrived in Knutsford in 1862, while the railway system in Italy was being built with the help of English engineers like Holdsworth at exactly the time of Lily's visits and of the writing of the story. The enthusiasm for the new culture of invention and industry reflects the Gaskells' friendships with people like James Nasmyth and the scientists and inventors who came to Manchester in 1861 for the annual meeting of the National Association for the Advancement of Science. But the central experiential allusion must be from Cousin Phillis herself to Meta. Meta too had loved and been let down by a man much more experienced in the ways of the world than she, and he too had left her for the other side of the globe. Her reaction had been, like Phillis, to struggle with psychosomatic illness, sometimes bringing her close to what Lily called 'hysteria'. To draw these analogies is not to say that the story is systematically biographical, but to suggest how, with a knowledge rooted in personal experience, Lily understood these things.

There was however a successful romance that followed the conclusion of *Cousin Phillis*. In July 1864 Lily received congratulations from George Smith on the engagement of Marianne to her cousin, Thurstan Holland. This courtship had been both protracted and difficult; Marianne and Thurstan had known each other since childhood, and the Gaskell family had long been accepted visitors at the Hollands' very grand home, Dumbleton Hall, in Worcestershire. Thurstan was interested in the question of social housing, one of Lily's philanthropic causes at this time; he was someone she would have approved of. But Edward Holland, his father, was a man very conscious of his social standing. Educated at Eton and Oxford, he had not only built his house at Dumbleton but had restored the estate that he had inherited from his father, Swinton Holland. From the outset he was opposed to the marriage, informing the Gaskells that as he had eleven other children Thurstan and Marianne could expect no financial support from him; furthermore the fact that they were cousins through the Holland line made marriage between them undesirable. But unlike the other Gaskell engagements this one does not seem to have been a matter of impulse. When Lily informed Norton of the match she reverted to the theme of the potential loss of a child: '*We* don't mind a long engagement for we shall keep our child that much the longer.' As for the child herself, now nearly thirty, 'the prospect of a long engagement does not seem to "tell" upon her at all.' In the end Thurstan's father came round, and Thurstan effectively became one of the Gaskell family from this point, proving himself invaluable, as will be seen, in times of crisis.

It was in that same summer of 1864 that Lily sent George Smith the outline of a new novel, 'a story… of country-town life 40 years ago'. She says she is planning it to take up 870 pages of her writing. She foresees three volumes, thus following the format of *Sylvia's Lovers*, adding that she has, as yet, no title for it. This new novel would replace an abandoned project that she refers to as the 'Two Mothers'; it first appeared in monthly instalments in *Cornhill*, again with illustrations by Du Maurier, under another title betokening relationship, *Wives and Daughters*.

The abandoned 'Two Mothers' and the accepted *Wives and Daughters* suggest Lily's preoccupations at this time. In the finished novel the 'wives' are the wife of Squire Hamley, concerned about her sons and her husband's attitudes to them, and Hyacinth Clare, otherwise Kirkpatrick, who becomes Dr Gibson's second wife; the 'daughters' are the motherless Molly Gibson and the fatherless Cynthia Kirkpatrick, who has suffered the consequences of her unsatisfactory upbringing by her self-interested mother. The title thus ignores the strongly drawn male characters, not only Doctor Gibson but the blustering Squire Hamley and his two sons, both public school and Cambridge educated. In the situation of the Hamley sons we see an early example of the issue of the two cultures: the elder, Osborne, is a poet of a somewhat Tennysonian kind, while his younger brother is on the verge of a distinguished scientific career.

The scientific references in *Wives and Daughters* indicate Lily's interest in the subject, not so much for its own sake perhaps but as an expression of a culture in action. In her visits to Oxford at this point in these later years she participated in university life, listening to lectures, dining at college luncheons, attending a Christ Church ball and worshipping at St Mary's. She met Matthew Arnold and Benjamin Jowett, together with distinguished scientists and mathematicians, and these contacts too would have brought her some understanding of the potential of the scientific culture. Her accounts of her Oxford visits carry something of the colour of her accounts of Rome: there is the same sense of excitement, and of a positive response to new people and new ideas. In *Wives and Daughters*, Roger Hamley is a research scientist, not unlike a younger Charles Darwin; Lily and Darwin were distant cousins and they seem to have met on more than one occasion. There is no evidence of Lily's having read Darwin's work, but *The Origin of Species* was published in 1859, and she would surely have been aware of its impact. Going right back, the work of William Stevenson, agronomist and experimental farmer, would have instilled in Lily a strong sense of the priorities of the practical. *Wives and Daughters* is subtitled 'an every-day story' but the days are those of 'forty years ago'. Like its predecessor, *Wives and Daughters* is not a disguised autobiography, but it is a work replete with autobiographical allusion.

Lily began writing *Wives and Daughters* in May 1864, checking with Smith at the outset, 'what day of the month *must* you have the next month's MSS to print, in case I am driven very hard?' She was indeed driven very hard, partly by the usual domestic anxieties, but most of all by a new and entirely unexpected project. Without telling William, she embarked on a plan to buy a house for him in anticipation of his retirement, which would then provide security for their unmarried daughters. The plan, as she defined it, was typically generous but was fraught with difficulty. Her concern for William, now sixty years old, had intensified over the years. Lily records that when at home he had become increasingly reclusive, spending much of his time in his study. He took holidays, but made it clear that he preferred to do so alone: 'He is depressed & uncomfortable & easily annoyed,' Lily wrote to Anne Robson in May 1865, although she continues rather revealingly that, 'he is *much* more cheerful & happy in his mind, than he used to be, when younger.' But William's associations all lay in the north of England. The houses that Lily inspected for her purpose were all in her preferred southern counties; it would have taken some persuading for William to relocate permanently. And while Lily and William were accustomed to living independent lives, it is remarkable that Lily should have been able to keep such a secret, not to mention the others who shared it. Perhaps, as Jenny Uglow suggests, the house could be seen as representing all that Lily had achieved in *her* life, the purchase of which she could rationalise by *her* gift of it to *him*.[19]

Nevertheless, she went ahead. On a practical level there were financial and legal difficulties. George Smith agreed to pay Lily

£2000 for the copyright of her novel, and then advanced her £1200 to enable her to finalise the purchase of the house. With a son-in-law and a potential son-in-law who were both lawyers she was helped through the legal complexities, but the question of inheritance was not an easy one. Under the law as it stood Lily could neither sign contracts nor dispose of her earned income without her husband's consent. The house would go to William in the event of Lily pre-deceasing him, but she wanted to be sure that it would ultimately be inherited by Meta and Julia, and was determined that it should not go to 'collateral relations of Mr Gaskell's'. Over this however, as the law stood, she had no control. Charles Crompton advised that it might be possible to arrange for the bequest to come to all four daughters, perhaps via the sons-in-law since that would guarantee male legatees.

Lily's plans made for a very hectic year in 1865. Family life had to continue, and everyone seems to have been affected by the stress. It is difficult to believe that William was not aware that something was afoot. 'I am feeling much dispirited about everybody's health,' Lily wrote. She takes tonics, suffers from insomnia, and worries about Meta, who had been subject to more crying fits, for which she is prescribed *'a great deal of meat to eat,'* and 'bitter beer'. Hearn has 'depression of spirits', and even Lion, the dog, is unwell. The drains at Plymouth Grove give off a foul smell, and Lily puts her lassitude down to this, instructing Marianne, holding the fort in Manchester while she goes to France, about the measures she must take. Lily took two trips to France, one to Paris and a shorter one to Dieppe; these would normally have restored her, but they seem to have had little effect. Several houses were inspected and rejected before Lily settled on The Lawn, an old house with a Georgian facade near Alton in Hampshire. According to Meta it was 'a small house', but this was a matter of degree: it had ten bedrooms and was set in four acres of ground. Then there was building work to be done; its 'hideous furniture' had to be replaced, and Meta was despatched to London to choose carpets and furnishings for her mother's approval. 'Oh dear! I *am* nearly killed, but the *stress* of every thing is nearly over,' Lily wrote to Marianne in September 1865 and, ominously, just before signing her letter, 'oh how *dead* I feel!'

Possession of The Lawn was taken late in 1865, and the problems seemed to be resolving themselves. The house was made ready for occupation and a tenant was obtained for the time, until they should need it. *Wives and Daughters* was a few pages short of completion. And then on Sunday 12th November 1865, in the middle of afternoon tea at The Lawn with Meta, Florence, Charles Crompton and Julia around her, and with the faithful Hearn in attendance, Lily collapsed on her sofa, dying quickly, according to those who were there, 'without pain or any struggle'. Her last intelligible word, we are told, was 'Rome'. Marianne, who had taken on so much family responsibility, was with her father in Manchester, and Charlie Crompton hastened to Plymouth Grove to tell William of his wife's death in a house of which he is supposed to have had no knowledge. It was Thurstan who supervised the removal of Lily's coffin to Knutsford where, five days after her death, she was buried. The following day Thurstan wrote to Charles Eliot Norton, paying his own tribute to 'that fresh intellect, that powerful imagination, that kindly interest that she took in everyone around her'.[20]

Lily's doctor attributed her death to 'disease of the heart'. But it is conceivable that she knew she was dying. She had never expected to live long and in those last days at Alton she had premonitions of her death. According to Isabella Green, their Knutsford friend, Lily said to Julia of the house, 'I don't expect to come and live here, but it will be ready for all of you.'[21] Was she aware that her headaches and general malaise may have been symptomatic of a much more serious and specific terminal condition? At the moment of her death just a few pages of *Wives and Daughters* remained to be written. Was the urgency that she had expressed about completing it similarly founded? Had she perhaps taken medical advice, and was this the real secret behind the determination to complete the purchase of the house and the writing of her novel? If these questions are answered in the affirmative, we must surely include outstanding courage amongst the many virtues of this resourceful, articulate and humanely sympathetic woman.

Afterwards

When the infant Willie Gaskell died in 1844, and was buried in what his mother called the 'dull, dreary chapel-yard at Warrington', the assumption was that his would become a family tomb. So much is clear from the placing of its inscription. But at some point a decision must have been taken that Lily would be buried at Knutsford, and she was followed there by William in 1884, by Julia in 1908, and by Meta in 1913. William had lived on at Plymouth Grove with Meta and Julia; he continued to carry out his duties at Cross Street until the last year of his life. Marianne, who married Thurstan Holland less than a year after Lily's death, was the only Gaskell daughter to have children and she lived the longest of them, dying in 1920 in her eighty-sixth year, having survived her husband by thirty-six years. Meta and Julia lived at Plymouth Grove until their deaths, involving themselves extensively in Manchester's cultural and educational life. Florence predeceased both her father and her husband; she died in 1881.

The decision to bring Lily back to Knutsford not only signified a return to the surroundings of her childhood, it came to define the nature of her literary reputation. Knutsford, after all, *was* Cranford, and *Cranford* had already become the work by which she was always identified, 'A work which seems to us manifestly destined in its modest way to become a classic', as Henry James defined it in a post-mortem review of *Wives and Daughters*.

Editions of *Cranford* multiplied on both sides of the Atlantic through the last decades of the nineteenth century. In the last two decades of the century there were at least thirty reprints of one kind or another. The most famous – and the most influential – was the volume brought out by Macmillan in 1891, with its introduction by Anne Thackeray Ritchie and its very mannered illustrations by Hugh Thomson, putting the characters of Lily's stories back into a kind of never-never land inhabited exclusively by old ladies in mob caps. There were school editions, abridgements, dramatic adaptations and translations, and these carried on well into the twentieth century in both Britain and the United States. A.W. Ward's eight-volume 'Knutsford' edition of the collected works, in its dark red binding with the Gaskell signature in gilt on the front cover, first published by Smith Elder in 1906, reinforced this view of Lily as a celebrant of a certain kind of literary decorum. Despite its inclusion of almost all of the novels and stories it did little to dispel Lily Gaskell's image as an author whose iconic work represented a particular strand of retrogressive Englishness. It was not until her work entered the academic canon after the Second World War, as a consequence of the identification of *Mary Barton* and *North and South* as contributions to the nineteenth-century 'condition of England' debate, that her reputation was revised to the point where she could take her place alongside her famous contemporaries. Her final works are now acknowledged as a further advance in her achievement: the novelist first recruited by Dickens occupies with equal success the fictional territory of George Eliot and the novelists of the 1860s. And in her diversity, both of kind and of quality, few novelists of her generation can be said to have been her equal. If her career has a complicated trajectory, this reflects the fact that she never wrote to a single overarching agenda, and she never told the same story twice. From the materials she provides for the biographer many different narratives can be told; they will all add to our understanding not only of her life but of the multiple contexts in which she lived and wrote.

Cranford's many dramatic adaptations – there were perhaps as many as fifty in Britain and the United States in the first half of the nineteenth century – have been followed by dramatisations on television. In a sense these can be seen as illustration come to life. There was a very early television adaptation of *Cranford* in 1951, and a four-part adaptation of *Cousin Phillis* (1982), and there were further televised productions of *Cranford* in 1972 and 1976. Most successful of all in bringing Lily's work to a modern audience was the large-scale adaptation of *Wives and Daughters* (BBC, 1999). This did a great deal to revive interests both biographical and literary; it was followed by *North and South* (ITV, 2005). Recently these have been followed by two more adaptations of *Cranford* by the BBC (2008, 2009); these included plot lines from other stories. This was not always successful, but they introduced their audience to the variety of Lily's work. The same nostalgia that ensured *Cranford*'s early success has tended to feed through into these visual representations, but it can fairly be said that Lily has been well served by the modern media; for better more than for worse it has brought her into the contemporary cultural consciousness and revealed the wider range of her achievement.

Notes

1. 'My Diary', reprinted in *Private Voices: The Diaries of Elizabeth Gaskell and Sophia Holland*, ed. J.A.V. Chapple and Anita Wilson (1996), p. 63.
2. Manuscript letters of William and John Stevenson are held in the J.G. Sharps collection, the John Rylands University Library of Manchester (JRULM).
3. John Chapple, *Elizabeth Gaskell: The Early Years* (1997), pp. 238–9.
4. Jenny Uglow, *Elizabeth Gaskell: A Habit of Stories* (1993), p. 35.
5. Chapple, *Early Years*, p. 425.
6. *Private Voices*, pp. 50–71.
7. Thomas Carlyle to Mrs Gaskell, 8th November 1848, ms letter held in JRULM.
8. Charlotte Brontë to Mrs Elizabeth Smith, 1st July 1851, *The Letters of Charlotte Brontë*, ed. Margaret Smith, 3 vols. (1995; 2000; 2004) vol. 2, p. 654.
9. Dickens to Gaskell, 31st January 1850, *The Pilgrim Edition of the Letters of Charles Dickens*, ed. Madeline House, Graham Storey and Kathleen Tillotson, 12 vols. (1965–2002), vol. 6, p. 22.
10. Unpublished letter held in JRULM.
11. Charlotte Brontë to Ellen Nussey, 21st December 1850, *Charlotte Brontë Letters*, vol. 2, p. 537
12. Charlotte Brontë to Gaskell 6th August 1851; 22nd May 1852, *Charlotte Brontë Letters*, vol. 2. p. 677; vol. 3, p. 48.
13. Angus Easson, *Elizabeth Gaskell: The Critical Heritage* (1991), pp. 200–319..
14. Dickens to Mrs Gaskell, 16th June 1854, *Dickens Letters*, vol. 7, p. 355.
15. Dickens to W.H. Wills, 19th August 1854; 14th October 1854, *Dickens Letters*, vol. 7, pp. 399, 439.
16. *Letters and Memorials of Catherine Winkworth* (1888), vol. 2, p. 109.
17. Margaret Lesser, *Clarkey: a Portrait in letters of Mary Clarke Mohl*, p. 169.
18. *Gaskell Society Newsletter*, no 14, August 1992.
19. Uglow, pp. 566–7.
20. *Gaskell Letters*, pp. 970–1
21. Ms letter held in JRULM.

List of works

Only works that have undisputed attribution have been included in this listing. Short works are in roman type; longer stories and novels in italic. *HW*: *Household Words*; *AYR*: *All the Year Round*; *CM*: *Cornhill Magazine*.

My Diary (1835–8, first published 1923)
'On Visiting the Grave of my Stillborn Little Girl'
(1836, unpublished poem)
'Sketches among the Poor,' No. 1 (*Blackwoods Magazine*, 1837)
'Clopton Hall' (1840)
'Libbie Marsh's Three Eras' (1847)
'The Sexton's Hero' (1847)
'Emerson's Lectures' (1847)
'Christmas Storms and Sunshine' (1848)
Mary Barton (1848)
'Hand and Heart' (1849)
'The Last Generation in England' (1849)
'Martha Preston' (1850)
'Lizzie Leigh' (*HW*, 1850)
'The Well of Pen-Morfa' (*HW*, 1850)
The Moorland Cottage (1850)
'The Heart of John Middleton (*HW*, 1850)
'Disappearances' (*HW*, 1851)
Cranford (*HW* 1851–3; 1853)
'Bessie's Troubles at Home' (1852)
'The Old Nurse's Story (*HW*, 1852)
'The Schah's English Gardener (*HW*, 1852)
Ruth (1853)
'Cumberland Sheep-Shearers' (*HW*, 1853)
'Bran' (*HW*, 1853)
'Morton Hall' (*HW*, 1853)
'Traits and Stories of the Huguenots' (*HW*, 1853)
'My French Master' (*HW*, 1853)

'The Squire's Story' (*HW*, 1853)
'The Scholar's Story' (*HW*, 1853)
'Modern Greek Songs' (*HW*, 1854)
'Company Manners' (*HW*, 1854)
North and South (*HW*, 1854–5, 1855)
'An Accursed Race' (*HW*, 1855)
'Half a Lifetime Ago' (*HW*, 1855)
'The Poor Clare' (*HW*, 1856)
Preface to *Mabel Vaughan* by Maria Cummins (1857)
'The Doom of the Griffiths' (1858)
'An Incident at Niagara Falls' (1858)
My Lady Ludlow (*HW*, 1858, in *Right at Last and Other Tales*, 1860)
'The Sin of a Father,' (*HW*, 1858), republished as *Right at Last*, 1860)
'The Manchester Marriage' (*HW*, 1858)
Round the Sofa (Chain narrative to allow for publication of a collection of otherwise unrelated stories) (1859)
'The Half-Brothers' (1859)
Lois the Witch (*AYR*, 1859)
'The Ghost in the Garden Room' (retitled 'The Crooked Branch' *AYR*, 1859)
'Curious if True'(*CM*, 1860)
The Grey Woman (*AYR*, 1861)
Preface to *Garibaldi at Caprera* by Colonel Vecchi (1862)
'Six Weeks at Heppenheim' (*CM*, 1862)
A Dark Night's Work (*AYR*, 1863)
Sylvia's Lovers (1863)
'An Italian Institution' (*AYR*, 1863)
Cousin Phillis (*CM*, 1863–4)
'Robert Gould Shaw' (*Macmillan's Magazine*, 1863)
'Crowley Castle' (*AYR*, 1863)
'French Life' (*Fraser's Magazine*, 1864)
Wives and Daughters (*CM*, 1864–6, 1866)

Further reading

Gaskell's complete works have been gathered in the collected edition published by Pickering and Chatto, general editor Joanne Shattock (2005–6). There are paperback reprints of individual works too numerous to specify. She has been fortunate in her biographers, although some have tended towards the hagiographic: she is after all a very sympathetic subject. An early example is Mrs Ellis Chadwick's *Mrs Gaskell: Haunts, Homes and Stories* (1910, rev. 1913). Its author had the advantage of contacts with direct knowledge of the Gaskell family. Annette B. Hopkins, *Elizabeth Gaskell: Her Life and Work* (1952), is thoroughly researched up to its date of publication. The outstanding modern biography is by Jenny Uglow, *Elizabeth Gaskell: A Habit of Stories* (1993). On Gaskell's early life J.A.V. Chapple, *Elizabeth Gaskell: the Early Years* (1997), is driven by its research into not only the young Gaskell, but also her various very complicated family connections: it is a masterpiece of detail. Essential primary sources are the two volumes of Gaskell's correspondence, *The Letters of Mrs Gaskell*, edited by John Chapple and Arthur Pollard (1966), and *Further Letters of Mrs Gaskell* (2000) edited by John Chapple and Alan Shelston, together with John Geoffrey Sharps' pioneering documentation of Gaskell's writing history, *Mrs Gaskell's Observation and Invention* (1966). Nancy S. Weyant's two bibliographies, *Elizabeth Gaskell: An Annotated Bibliography of English Sources, 1976–1991* (1994) and *1992–2001* (2004) are invaluable. My debt to these writers and scholars, in this study and elsewhere, cannot be measured. *Letters and Memorials of Catherine Winkworth* (2 vols., 1888) contains much detailed biographical information, but it is now unfortunately virtually inaccessible. The *Letters of Charlotte Brontë* (vol. 1, 1995; vol. 2, 2000; vol. 3, 2004), edited by Margaret Smith, document the Gaskell–Brontë connection. Graham Handley's *An Elizabeth Gaskell Chronology* charts the daily course of its subject's life. It has been invaluable in the compilation of this 'Brief Life'.

Gaskell criticism perhaps has a less coherent history. A comprehensive collection of nineteenth-century responses can be found in Angus Easson's *Elizabeth Gaskell: The Critical Heritage* (1991). Criticism entered its modern phase with Edgar Wright's *Mrs Gaskell: the Basis for Re-Assessment* (1965): since then Patsy Stoneman's feminist study *Elizabeth Gaskell* (1987) has covered the full range of the works with great sympathy. Hilary D. Schor, *Scheherezade in the Market Place*, and Felicia Bonaparte, *The Gypsy-Bachelor of Manchester* (both 1992) take approaches that can fairly be described as non-traditional with varying degrees of effect. Linda K. Hughes and Michael Lund, *Victorian Publishing and Mrs Gaskell's Work* (1999), takes its critical stance from the context of publishing history. Terence Wright, *Elizabeth Gaskell: 'We are not angels'* (1995), is a sympathetic close reading of selected works. Shirley Foster, *Elizabeth Gaskell: A Literary Life* (2002), concentrates on the work as I have concentrated on the life. Much Gaskell criticism is contained in articles, and non-specific studies of nineteenth-century fiction; many of the articles can be found, with the aid of Weyant's bibliographies, in *The Gaskell Society Journal*, vols. 1 (1987) to 22 (2008).

Biographical note

Alan Shelston is Honorary Senior Research Fellow at the John Rylands Library, the University of Manchester, having been Senior Lecturer in English Literature at the University itself. He participated frequently in seminars at the Centro Universitario di Studi Vittoriani e Edoardiani at Pescara University in Italy. His publications include *Further Letters of Mrs Gaskell* (with John Chapple, 2000) and numerous essays on Gaskell's work. He has also published work on Dickens, on Hardy and on Henry James. He is President of the Gaskell Society.

HESPERUS PRESS

Hesperus Press is committed to bringing near what is far – far both in space and time. Works written by the greatest authors, and unjustly neglected or simply little known in the English-speaking world, are made accessible through new translations and a completely fresh editorial approach. Through these classic works, the reader is introduced to the greatest writers from all times and all cultures.

For more information on Hesperus Press, please visit our website: **www.hesperuspress.com**